The Inventory Optimization Handbook

Strategies, Techniques, and Tools for Modern Supply Chains

The Inventory Optimization Handbook
Strategies, Techniques, and Tools for Modern Supply Chains

Part 1: Foundations of Inventory Optimization

Chapter 1: Introduction to Inventory Optimization   6
Chapter 2: Fundamentals of Inventory Management   12
Chapter 3: Challenges in Inventory Optimization   18

Part 2: Inventory Analysis Techniques

Chapter 4: ABC Analysis   25
Chapter 5: XYZ Analysis   32
Chapter 6: Pareto Principle in Inventory Management   39
Chapter 7: Advanced Inventory Categorization Methods   46

Part 3: Inventory Forecasting

Chapter 8: The Role of Demand Forecasting   55
Chapter 9: Forecasting Techniques   58
Chapter 10: Tools and Software for Inventory Forecasting   65

Part 4: Inventory Control Systems

Chapter 11: Push and Pull Inventory Systems   73
Chapter 12: Reorder Systems for Inventory Control   81
Chapter 13: Advanced Inventory Models   88

Part 5: Optimizing Stock Levels

Chapter 14: Safety Stock Management   95

Chapter 15: Inventory Rationalization Strategies		102

Part 6: Inventory Optimization Strategies

Chapter 16: Lean Inventory Management		110
Chapter 17: Agile Inventory Strategies		117
Chapter 18: Hybrid Inventory Strategies		124

Part 7: Leveraging Technology for Inventory Optimization

Chapter 19: ERP Systems and Inventory Management		132
Chapter 20: IoT and Smart Inventory Tracking		138
Chapter 21: AI and Machine Learning in Inventory Optimization		144

Part 8: Sustainability and Risk Management

Chapter 23: Sustainable Inventory Practices		151
Chapter 24: Risk Management in Inventory Optimization		158

Part 9: Specialized Topics in Inventory Management

Chapter 25: Inventory Metrics and KPIs		165
Chapter 26: Managing Non-Moving and Slow-Moving Inventory		172
Chapter 27: Raw Material Aging Reports and Burn-Off Reports 181
Chapter 28: Combining ABC and XYZ Analysis		188

Part 10: The Future of Inventory Optimization

Chapter 29: Emerging Trends in Inventory Management   195
Chapter 30: Preparing for the Next Generation of Inventory Challenges   201

Conclusion   208

Part 1: Foundations of Inventory Optimization

Chapter 1: Introduction to Inventory Optimization

Understanding Inventory Optimization

Inventory optimization refers to the process of managing and controlling inventory levels in a way that aligns with the goals and operational demands of a business. It is about finding the ideal balance between having enough stock to meet customer demand and not overstocking, which can lead to high holding costs and inventory waste. Essentially, it involves determining the right quantity of stock at the right time in the right place to ensure smooth operations, maximize profitability, and maintain excellent customer service.

Inventory optimization is not simply about reducing inventory levels to save costs; rather, it focuses on making sure that the business holds the optimal amount of inventory that will enable it to fulfill customer orders without delays while also minimizing carrying costs. This practice is vital across various industries, including retail, manufacturing, and distribution, where the ability to balance supply with demand can significantly impact a company's bottom line.

There are several components to inventory optimization, including demand forecasting, inventory categorization, reorder systems, and safety stock management. Each of these elements contributes to ensuring that businesses can effectively meet demand without excess stock, which is a key driver of cost reduction. In this sense, inventory optimization is not just about maintaining efficient stock levels, but also about improving operational efficiency, enhancing customer satisfaction, and reducing waste.

Importance in Supply Chain Management

Inventory optimization plays a central role in effective supply chain management. In any supply chain, inventory is a crucial asset that ties together various stages of the production and distribution process. Proper inventory management ensures that the right materials are available at the right time, thereby enabling the smooth flow of goods from suppliers to manufacturers and ultimately to end customers.

In the context of supply chain management, inventory optimization helps in several key areas. First, it helps in ensuring that production is not hindered due to material shortages. By maintaining the right amount of raw materials and work-in-progress inventory, manufacturers can keep production lines running smoothly. Similarly, for distributors and retailers, having optimized inventory levels means that customer demand can be met without unnecessary delays or stockouts, which ultimately enhances customer satisfaction and loyalty.

Additionally, inventory optimization is essential for maintaining cash flow. Excess inventory ties up capital that could otherwise be invested in other areas of the business, such as expanding operations, developing new products, or improving infrastructure. Efficient inventory management ensures that businesses can release working capital by reducing overstocking, thus freeing up resources for growth opportunities.

The growing complexity of global supply chains has made inventory optimization even more important. With multiple suppliers, distribution centers, and varying lead times, companies need to ensure that their inventory levels are not only adequate but also flexible enough to adapt to fluctuations in demand and supply chain disruptions. In today's world of just-in-time production, e-commerce, and rapidly changing customer preferences, inventory optimization is key to maintaining a competitive edge.

Key Goals and Challenges

The primary goal of inventory optimization is to balance demand with supply while minimizing costs and maximizing customer satisfaction. However, achieving this balance is not a simple task. It involves a series of interconnected processes that require a detailed understanding of demand patterns, supply chain dynamics, and the financial implications of inventory decisions.

One of the most important goals of inventory optimization is minimizing stockouts and overstock situations. A stockout occurs when the inventory level is insufficient to meet customer demand, leading to lost sales, customer dissatisfaction, and potential damage to the brand's reputation. On the other hand, overstocking can lead to high holding costs, excess inventory that may become obsolete, and inefficient use of storage space. Therefore, businesses need to determine the right reorder points and optimal inventory levels to avoid these extremes.

Another critical goal of inventory optimization is improving inventory turnover. Inventory turnover refers to the rate at which inventory is sold and replaced over a given period. A higher turnover rate typically indicates that a business is effectively managing its inventory by selling products quickly and efficiently. Conversely, low inventory turnover can indicate overstocking or poor sales, both of which can negatively impact profitability. The goal is to find a turnover rate that aligns with business needs while also ensuring that there is enough stock to meet customer demand.

To achieve these goals, businesses must continually monitor and analyze their inventory performance. This requires real-time tracking of inventory levels, sales data, and demand forecasting accuracy. With the right systems and technologies in place, businesses can adjust their strategies to account for fluctuations in demand, market conditions, and supply chain disruptions.

While the goals of inventory optimization are clear, businesses face numerous challenges in trying to achieve them. One of the biggest challenges is demand variability. Demand for products is rarely constant; it fluctuates based on seasonal trends, promotions, market conditions, and consumer preferences. Businesses must accurately forecast demand to avoid either excess inventory or stockouts. However, demand forecasting is not always straightforward, as unpredictable factors such as economic downturns, weather events, or shifts in consumer behavior can dramatically alter demand patterns.

Supply chain disruptions also pose a significant challenge to inventory optimization. Global supply chains are vulnerable to a range of risks, including natural disasters, political instability, and transportation delays. These disruptions can lead to delays in receiving goods from suppliers, which in turn affects inventory levels and the ability to meet customer demand. For businesses to optimize their inventory, they must have contingency plans in place to deal with these disruptions, including maintaining strategic safety stock levels or finding alternative suppliers to mitigate risks.

Technology also plays a central role in inventory optimization, but integrating new systems and tools can be a challenge for many businesses. Many companies still rely on outdated manual processes or basic software systems that do not provide the level of accuracy and visibility needed to effectively manage inventory. The adoption of advanced inventory management systems, such as Enterprise Resource Planning (ERP) systems or cloud-based solutions, can improve real-time inventory tracking, demand forecasting, and order processing, but it requires significant investment and training. Furthermore, businesses must integrate these systems with other supply chain technologies, such as warehouse management systems (WMS) and transportation management systems (TMS), to ensure seamless operations.

Data management is another challenge in inventory optimization. To make informed decisions, businesses must collect and analyze large amounts of data related to inventory levels, sales patterns, supplier performance, and market trends. Without robust data management practices, businesses may struggle to extract meaningful insights that can inform inventory decisions. Moreover, data accuracy is critical, as incorrect or outdated information can lead to poor inventory decisions and, ultimately, financial losses.

Finally, businesses must constantly reassess and adjust their inventory optimization strategies to stay competitive. Consumer expectations are evolving, and e-commerce has introduced new challenges, such as the demand for faster shipping and more flexible delivery options. In this environment, companies must continuously optimize their inventory to meet customer expectations while maintaining profitability. This requires a combination of agile inventory management techniques, effective use of technology, and the ability to respond quickly to changes in the market and the supply chain.

In conclusion, inventory optimization is a complex and multifaceted process that plays a crucial role in the success of supply chain management. It involves understanding the right balance between demand and supply, minimizing costs, and maximizing customer satisfaction. While businesses face significant challenges in achieving optimal inventory levels, the benefits of doing so are substantial. Through advanced forecasting techniques, efficient reorder systems, and the strategic use of technology, companies can overcome these challenges and ensure that their inventory management practices support their broader business objectives.

Chapter 2: Fundamentals of Inventory Management

Types of Inventory (Raw Materials, Work-In-Progress, Finished Goods)

Inventory management is a key aspect of supply chain operations, and understanding the different types of inventory is fundamental for effective management. There are three primary types of inventory in most manufacturing and retail operations: raw materials, work-in-progress (WIP), and finished goods. Each of these types plays a distinct role in the production process and impacts a company's financial performance in unique ways.

Raw Materials refer to the basic materials that are used to manufacture products. These are the inputs that are processed or assembled into finished products. Raw materials can include everything from metal, plastic, and wood to more specialized components like microchips or fabric. Raw materials are typically purchased from suppliers and stored until they are needed in the production process. The management of raw materials is crucial because delays in procurement can halt production, while overstocking can increase storage costs and reduce liquidity.

Work-In-Progress (WIP) inventory represents the goods that are in the process of being manufactured but are not yet complete. These items are partially finished, having undergone one or more stages of production, but are not ready for sale. WIP inventory is vital for ensuring a continuous flow of goods in manufacturing environments. Managing WIP involves balancing the need to keep production moving while preventing unnecessary accumulation, which can tie up capital. Too much WIP can indicate inefficiencies in the production process, while too little can result in production delays.

Finished Goods are the final products that are completed and ready for sale. These are the items that have passed through all stages of production and are now available for distribution to customers. In retail or wholesale settings, finished goods inventory can include products such as electronics, clothing, or packaged food. Finished goods inventory is critical for meeting customer demand and ensuring timely delivery. Managing this inventory involves forecasting demand accurately to avoid both stockouts and excess inventory. Finished goods represent the highest level of inventory in the supply chain, as they are ready to be sold or shipped to customers.

Each of these types of inventory plays a crucial role in the overall inventory management strategy. A well-optimized system ensures that raw materials are available for production when needed, WIP inventory is managed efficiently to avoid bottlenecks, and finished goods are stocked in the right quantities to meet customer demand without overstocking.

Inventory Costs and Financial Impact (Holding, Ordering, Shortage Costs)

Inventory management is not just about maintaining the right levels of stock; it is also about understanding and minimizing the costs associated with holding, ordering, and facing shortages. These costs can significantly impact a company's profitability and cash flow, making it essential for businesses to carefully balance inventory levels to avoid unnecessary expenditures.

Holding Costs (also known as carrying costs) represent the expenses associated with storing inventory. These costs include warehousing expenses, insurance, utilities, taxes, and depreciation of inventory. The longer inventory stays in storage, the higher the holding costs. For businesses that deal with large volumes of inventory or perishable goods, holding costs can quickly add up. Minimizing holding costs is a key goal in inventory management, as excessive inventory ties up capital that could be invested elsewhere. Therefore, companies strive to optimize inventory levels to avoid both stockouts and overstocking, which would increase holding costs.

In addition to the physical costs of storage, holding inventory can also result in opportunity costs. Money spent on storing inventory is money that could have been used for other investments or operational needs, such as purchasing new equipment, expanding production capacity, or increasing marketing efforts. Thus, it is critical to maintain an inventory level that balances operational needs with cost efficiency.

Ordering Costs are incurred each time an order is placed with a supplier to replenish inventory. These costs include the administrative expenses of creating and processing orders, transportation costs, and any other fees associated with receiving goods, such as customs duties and inspection charges. While ordering costs are typically lower than holding costs, they can still add up, particularly for businesses that make frequent orders for smaller quantities. This is why many companies seek to minimize ordering costs by ordering in larger quantities, though this must be balanced against holding costs.

Shortage Costs arise when inventory is insufficient to meet customer demand, resulting in stockouts. A stockout can lead to lost sales, delayed deliveries, and potentially lost customers. The shortage costs can include lost revenue, expedited shipping to fulfill backorders, and reputational damage. The financial impact of stockouts can be significant, as customers who experience delays may turn to competitors, which can lead to a longer-term loss of business. Companies may also face penalties for failing to deliver goods on time, further increasing costs. Therefore, maintaining a sufficient level of safety stock to mitigate the risks of stockouts is a critical aspect of inventory management. However, businesses must balance this with the risk of overstocking, which incurs its own set of costs.

Inventory Turnover Ratio and Service Levels

The **Inventory Turnover Ratio** is a key performance indicator (KPI) used to measure the efficiency of inventory management. It is calculated by dividing the cost of goods sold (COGS) by the average inventory during a specific period. The formula is:

$$\text{Inventory Turnover Ratio} = \frac{\text{Cost of Goods Sold (COGS)}}{\text{Average Inventory}}$$

A high inventory turnover ratio indicates that a company is selling and replenishing inventory quickly, which is generally considered a positive sign of operational efficiency. It suggests that products are in demand, inventory is being managed well, and the company is effectively converting its stock into sales. A low turnover ratio, on the other hand, can signal overstocking, slow sales, or poor inventory management.

The inventory turnover ratio is closely tied to cash flow, as businesses with high turnover rates are able to sell goods quickly and generate revenue, freeing up capital to reinvest in the business. However, it is important to interpret the turnover ratio in context, as industries with perishable goods or rapid product cycles typically have higher turnover rates than those that deal with durable goods or high-value items that take longer to sell.

Another important concept related to inventory turnover is **Service Levels**. Service level refers to the ability of a company to meet customer demand without experiencing stockouts. A high service level means that a business is able to fulfill orders promptly and maintain a positive customer experience. Service level is typically expressed as a percentage of demand met from available inventory. A company may aim for a high service level to ensure that customers receive their orders on time, but this must be balanced against the costs of maintaining higher inventory levels, which could increase holding costs.

Maintaining an optimal service level involves forecasting demand accurately and having the right amount of inventory on hand to meet that demand. Service levels are often adjusted based on factors such as customer expectations, product seasonality, and lead times from suppliers. In some cases, businesses may accept a slightly lower service level in exchange for reducing inventory levels and associated holding costs. However, companies must carefully evaluate the trade-off between service levels and inventory costs, as poor service levels can lead to dissatisfied customers and lost business.

In conclusion, the fundamentals of inventory management are critical for any organization looking to optimize its operations. Understanding the types of inventory—raw materials, work-in-progress, and finished goods—along with the costs associated with holding, ordering, and facing shortages, is essential for effective decision-making. Additionally, measuring performance through metrics like inventory turnover ratio and managing service levels are crucial for maintaining balance between efficient operations and customer satisfaction. By strategically managing inventory, companies can not only reduce costs but also improve their overall supply chain efficiency, leading to better financial outcomes and enhanced competitiveness.

Chapter 3: Challenges in Inventory Optimization

Effective inventory optimization is essential for maintaining a smooth and efficient supply chain. However, various challenges can disrupt the delicate balance required for optimizing inventory. These challenges stem from a variety of sources, such as demand variability, supply chain disruptions, and internal barriers within organizations, including technological constraints. Addressing these challenges requires a proactive approach, advanced planning, and the use of modern tools and strategies to ensure that inventory is neither overstocked nor understocked. Below are some of the key challenges organizations face when striving to achieve optimal inventory levels.

Demand Variability

One of the most significant challenges in inventory optimization is demand variability. Demand for products can fluctuate unpredictably, influenced by various factors such as seasonal trends, economic conditions, consumer preferences, and external events like promotions or market disruptions. This variability makes it difficult for companies to accurately forecast demand and maintain appropriate inventory levels.

When demand is stable and predictable, inventory management can be relatively straightforward. However, in environments where demand is highly variable, companies must contend with the risk of either overstocking or understocking. Overstocking can lead to increased holding costs, inventory obsolescence, and wasted resources. On the other hand, understocking results in stockouts, which can lead to lost sales, customer dissatisfaction, and potentially damaged reputations.

Managing demand variability requires advanced demand forecasting techniques and tools. These can include statistical methods, machine learning models, and demand sensing technologies that use real-time data to predict changes in demand more accurately. Companies can also implement safety stock strategies or adopt demand-driven inventory practices, where inventory levels are adjusted based on actual demand rather than relying solely on historical data.

However, even with advanced forecasting methods, demand variability remains a persistent challenge. For instance, unexpected spikes in demand (such as during holidays or promotional events) or sudden downturns in market conditions can create significant inventory challenges. To cope with such variability, businesses often use agile inventory strategies that allow them to adjust quickly and efficiently to changes in demand patterns.

Supply Chain Disruptions

Supply chain disruptions are another major challenge to effective inventory optimization. These disruptions can occur due to a wide range of factors, including natural disasters, geopolitical instability, labor strikes, transportation delays, or even a breakdown in relationships with key suppliers. Any disruption in the supply chain can cause delays in the delivery of raw materials, intermediate goods, or finished products, leading to stockouts or backlogs.

The impact of supply chain disruptions on inventory management can be severe. For example, if a critical component from a supplier is delayed, production might have to stop, leading to a shortage of finished goods and potential customer dissatisfaction. Furthermore, if companies have insufficient inventory buffers or fail to diversify their supply sources, they may find themselves in a vulnerable position when disruptions occur.

To mitigate the risks associated with supply chain disruptions, businesses need to develop robust risk management strategies. This can include identifying potential vulnerabilities in the supply chain, maintaining strategic partnerships with multiple suppliers, and implementing dual-sourcing or multi-sourcing strategies. Additionally, companies should invest in supply chain visibility technologies that provide real-time updates on inventory levels, supplier performance, and transportation status, allowing them to quickly detect and respond to disruptions.

Supply chain disruptions also necessitate the establishment of contingency plans that can be activated in case of emergencies. These plans should outline the steps to be taken when disruptions occur, such as sourcing alternative suppliers, prioritizing high-demand products, or utilizing expedited shipping to meet customer demands.

Organizational and Technological Barriers

While external factors like demand variability and supply chain disruptions pose significant challenges, internal organizational and technological barriers can also impede effective inventory optimization. These barriers often stem from a lack of coordination between departments, outdated processes, or insufficient technology.

From an organizational perspective, inventory management is often siloed, with different teams responsible for procurement, production, and sales. These departments may not always communicate effectively, leading to a disconnect between inventory planning and actual demand. For example, the procurement team may order large quantities of raw materials based on historical forecasts, while the sales team may know that demand is trending lower than expected. This misalignment can result in overstocking or understocking, neither of which is ideal for business operations.

To overcome these organizational challenges, businesses must foster better cross-functional collaboration. Inventory management should be viewed as a company-wide responsibility, with frequent communication and information sharing between all stakeholders involved. Companies can establish integrated planning processes that involve key decision-makers from procurement, production, logistics, and sales to ensure that inventory decisions are aligned with actual demand.

On the technological front, many businesses still rely on legacy systems for inventory management, which can be inefficient and unable to handle the complexities of modern supply chains. Outdated software may lack real-time tracking capabilities, automated replenishment features, or predictive analytics tools that can improve forecasting accuracy and inventory optimization.

Investing in modern technology is essential for overcoming these barriers. Advanced inventory management systems (IMS), Enterprise Resource Planning (ERP) systems, and supply chain management platforms enable real-time tracking of inventory levels, better demand forecasting, and automated decision-making. These technologies also integrate with other business systems, allowing for seamless data flow across departments. By implementing cutting-edge technology, companies can improve their inventory management processes and respond more effectively to changes in demand or supply chain disruptions.

Another technological challenge lies in the complexity of data management. In today's data-driven world, businesses have access to vast amounts of information, including sales data, supplier performance metrics, and customer feedback. However, without the proper tools to analyze and interpret this data, companies may struggle to make informed inventory decisions. The implementation of data analytics, machine learning algorithms, and artificial intelligence (AI) can help businesses leverage this data to optimize inventory levels and enhance decision-making.

Conclusion

Inventory optimization is essential for maintaining a competitive edge in today's dynamic business environment. However, companies face numerous challenges in achieving the ideal balance between supply and demand. Demand variability, supply chain disruptions, and organizational and technological barriers can all complicate inventory management efforts. To navigate these challenges successfully, businesses must adopt a proactive and strategic approach, leveraging advanced forecasting tools, improving supply chain resilience, and investing in modern technology to enhance visibility and efficiency. By overcoming these challenges, companies can optimize their inventory levels, reduce costs, and improve customer satisfaction, ultimately driving profitability and long-term success.

Part 2: Inventory Analysis Techniques

Chapter 4: ABC Analysis

Inventory management is an essential function of any business, as it directly impacts both operational efficiency and customer satisfaction. One of the most widely used techniques for managing inventory is the ABC analysis, a method that classifies inventory into different categories based on their value and importance to the business. By understanding the key principles of ABC analysis, organizations can focus their resources and efforts on managing the most critical inventory items, improving inventory control, and enhancing overall supply chain performance. This chapter delves into the basics of ABC categorization and its applications in inventory management.

Basics of ABC Categorization

ABC analysis is based on the Pareto Principle, also known as the 80/20 rule, which asserts that a small percentage of items in an inventory typically contribute to the majority of value or impact. The basic premise of ABC analysis is to categorize inventory items into three groups—A, B, and C—based on their importance to the business. These categories are determined by evaluating each item's contribution to overall sales or profit, as well as factors like demand frequency and cost.

> **Category A:** This group consists of the most critical and valuable inventory items. These items represent a small percentage of the total inventory but account for the majority of the value or sales. Typically, about 10-20% of inventory items fall into this category, but they might contribute 70-80% of the total value or revenue. As a result, items in this category require close monitoring, frequent stock replenishment, and careful management to ensure they are available when needed.

Category B: Category B items are of moderate value and importance. They make up a larger portion of the inventory than Category A items, but they contribute a smaller share to the overall value or revenue. These items are typically given moderate attention and may require periodic reviews to ensure optimal inventory levels. About 30-40% of inventory items often fall into this category, contributing 10-20% of the overall value.

Category C: Category C items are low in value and account for the largest portion of inventory. However, these items have the least significant impact on overall revenue or sales. They are often characterized by low turnover rates or infrequent demand. Although they comprise the bulk of inventory items (typically 50-60%), Category C items contribute only a small percentage of total value (often 5-10%). These items require less frequent monitoring, as they do not significantly affect overall business performance.

The key to effective ABC analysis is not just categorizing inventory, but using this information to prioritize resources and focus efforts on managing the most valuable items. By applying the 80/20 rule, businesses can allocate resources in a way that minimizes stockouts of high-value items while reducing the costs associated with carrying low-value items.

Applications in Inventory Management

ABC analysis is a highly effective technique for inventory management that allows businesses to optimize their inventory control efforts and improve operational efficiency. Below are some key applications of ABC analysis in inventory management:

1. Prioritizing Stock Control Efforts

One of the most direct applications of ABC analysis is in prioritizing stock control efforts. By identifying which items have the greatest impact on sales or profitability, businesses can allocate more resources to ensuring that high-value items (Category A) are always in stock and available for customers. These items may require more frequent reordering, safety stock, and closer supplier relationships to ensure availability.

In contrast, lower-value items in Category C can be managed with less frequency and effort. Organizations may choose to keep lower safety stock levels, order these items less often, or even discontinue them if they do not contribute significantly to the business. This enables businesses to optimize their inventory levels, reduce carrying costs, and improve cash flow.

2. Inventory Replenishment Strategies

ABC analysis can also help in developing effective inventory replenishment strategies. For Category A items, businesses often use just-in-time (JIT) inventory systems or make frequent orders to keep inventory levels low while ensuring that stockouts are avoided. Because these items represent a high percentage of sales, stockouts can lead to significant lost revenue and customer dissatisfaction.

For Category B items, a more moderate replenishment approach may be appropriate. Businesses can use reorder point systems that trigger automatic reordering when inventory reaches a certain threshold. These items are less critical than Category A items, but ensuring they remain in stock is still important for maintaining steady sales and operational efficiency.

Category C items, on the other hand, may require less sophisticated replenishment methods. In many cases, businesses may decide to only reorder these items when demand arises, or they may choose to hold limited stock to minimize carrying costs. For products that are not frequently purchased, it may be beneficial to rely on suppliers with shorter lead times to reduce the need for holding large amounts of stock.

3. Reducing Stockouts and Overstocking

Effective inventory management is all about finding the right balance between stockouts and overstocking. ABC analysis helps businesses achieve this balance by ensuring that the most critical items are always in stock and available for customers while preventing the overstocking of low-value items that consume unnecessary resources.

For Category A items, businesses should prioritize reducing stockouts and ensuring that these items are always available. Having real-time visibility into stock levels and demand trends is critical for making informed decisions about when to reorder these high-value products. On the other hand, for Category C items, companies can afford to have occasional stockouts without significantly impacting customer satisfaction or revenue. By using ABC analysis to identify these items, companies can avoid overstocking and reduce their inventory carrying costs.

4. Optimizing Warehouse Space

Warehouse space is often limited and costly, so it is important to optimize storage based on the value and demand of inventory items. ABC analysis plays a significant role in warehouse optimization by helping businesses prioritize storage for high-value items. Category A items, being the most critical, should be placed in prime locations within the warehouse to facilitate faster picking and replenishment.

Category B items can be stored in less accessible areas but still organized for relatively efficient picking. Category C items, which are low in value and have lower demand, can be stored in more remote areas or in larger quantities to maximize space utilization without taking up prime locations in the warehouse.

By using ABC analysis to guide warehouse layout decisions, businesses can improve efficiency, reduce picking time, and ensure that space is used in a way that aligns with the business's inventory needs.

5. Supplier Relationship Management

ABC analysis can also assist in supplier relationship management. Category A items, which are the most critical and high-value, often require reliable suppliers with strong performance records and the ability to provide products on time. Businesses may choose to negotiate more favorable terms, such as better payment options, shorter lead times, or priority service for these items to ensure that they are always available when needed.

For Category B items, businesses can work with a broader range of suppliers, using multiple sources to ensure consistency and cost-effectiveness. For Category C items, businesses may consider working with low-cost suppliers or consolidating orders to minimize overhead while ensuring that stock levels remain sufficient to meet demand.

Conclusion

ABC analysis is a powerful inventory management technique that helps businesses prioritize inventory control efforts based on the value and importance of their stock. By categorizing items into A, B, and C groups, businesses can allocate resources more effectively, optimize their replenishment strategies, reduce stockouts and overstocking, and improve warehouse efficiency. The key to success with ABC analysis lies in understanding the value of each inventory item and ensuring that management efforts align with the business's strategic goals. When implemented correctly, ABC analysis can drive significant improvements in inventory management, contributing to better profitability, operational efficiency, and customer satisfaction.

Chapter 5: XYZ Analysis

In the field of inventory management, businesses are constantly seeking new ways to improve inventory control and optimize stock levels. One such approach is XYZ analysis, a technique that complements traditional methods like ABC analysis. XYZ analysis focuses on the consumption patterns of inventory items, providing valuable insights into their demand behavior. By understanding how frequently and predictably items are consumed, businesses can make more informed decisions about inventory stocking, replenishment, and risk management. This chapter explores the concept of XYZ analysis and its integration with ABC analysis to form a powerful tool for advanced inventory categorization.

Understanding Consumption Patterns

Unlike ABC analysis, which classifies inventory items based on their monetary value, XYZ analysis categorizes items based on their consumption patterns—how regularly they are used or sold, and how predictable their demand is over time. The primary objective of XYZ analysis is to identify the variability in the consumption of items, which can directly influence decisions regarding inventory levels, order frequency, and stockouts.

The categorization in XYZ analysis is based on the following three levels:

> **X Category (Stable Consumption):** Items in the X category exhibit stable and predictable demand. Their consumption is relatively constant, and demand follows a consistent trend with little fluctuation over time. These items are typically easy to forecast, and the risk of stockouts or overstocking is low, making them ideal candidates for streamlined inventory management systems. For businesses, X items are often the most

reliable and can be replenished on a regular schedule with minimal disruption to operations.

Y Category (Moderate Fluctuation in Demand): Y items are characterized by moderate demand variability. Their consumption is somewhat predictable, but demand may fluctuate due to seasonality, promotions, or other factors. While not as stable as Category X, the demand for Y items can generally be forecasted with a moderate level of confidence. Businesses need to use flexible inventory management strategies for these items, as demand can spike unexpectedly or dip below forecasted levels. Effective safety stock strategies are essential to reduce the risk of stockouts while preventing excess inventory buildup.

Z Category (Highly Variable Demand): Items in the Z category experience erratic and unpredictable demand. Their consumption can fluctuate drastically, making it difficult to forecast future needs accurately. These items are often subject to market trends, external events, or unanticipated consumer behavior that can cause sharp demand spikes or declines. Businesses face higher risks when managing Z items, as stockouts or overstocking can have severe consequences. To manage Z items, organizations need to adopt highly flexible, agile inventory strategies that can quickly respond to changing demand patterns.

By understanding these consumption patterns, businesses can tailor their inventory management strategies to each category. For example, stable X items may benefit from a just-in-time (JIT) inventory system that minimizes carrying costs, while Y items may require safety stock buffers to manage demand fluctuations. Z items, on the other hand, may need a more dynamic approach, such as implementing demand sensing technology or closely monitoring market trends.

Combining XYZ with ABC for Advanced Categorization

While XYZ analysis focuses on demand variability, ABC analysis categorizes inventory based on value and importance to the business. However, when combined, these two techniques provide a more comprehensive approach to inventory management, allowing businesses to develop advanced categorization systems that address both the value and demand patterns of their inventory items. The integration of ABC and XYZ analysis enables organizations to make more strategic decisions about inventory replenishment, ordering, and storage, ensuring that critical items are always available while minimizing the costs associated with overstocking or understocking.

The combined categorization can be visualized as a two-dimensional matrix, where items are classified into nine distinct categories, based on their value (ABC) and demand behavior (XYZ). Each combination of ABC and XYZ classification represents a unique inventory management challenge and strategy. Here is how the nine categories can be interpreted:

> **AX (High Value, Stable Demand):** These items are of high value and have stable, predictable demand. They are critical to the business and should be managed with utmost care. These items require frequent replenishment to ensure availability but can be ordered in predictable patterns, keeping stockouts to a minimum.
>
> **AY (High Value, Moderate Fluctuation in Demand):** These items are high in value, but their demand can fluctuate. A flexible inventory management strategy is needed for these items, taking into account seasonal variations or promotional periods. Safety stock

levels should be adjusted accordingly to prevent stockouts during demand spikes while avoiding excessive inventory buildup during slower periods.

AZ (High Value, Highly Variable Demand): High-value items with highly unpredictable demand require careful attention. The business must adopt dynamic and agile inventory strategies to respond to demand fluctuations. These items may benefit from demand forecasting models or even advanced tools like machine learning algorithms to better predict demand and optimize inventory levels.

BX (Moderate Value, Stable Demand): These items are of moderate value and have stable consumption patterns. They are important but not as critical as Category A items. Businesses can manage these items with regular replenishment cycles, optimizing stock levels while minimizing carrying costs. These items can be ordered on a periodic basis without the need for extensive monitoring.

BY (Moderate Value, Moderate Fluctuation in Demand): These items have moderate value and experience fluctuations in demand. Inventory management for these items requires flexibility, such as using reorder point systems or safety stock calculations. These items may also benefit from trend analysis and demand forecasting, helping to anticipate periods of higher or lower demand.

BZ (Moderate Value, Highly Variable Demand): Items in this category are of moderate value but face significant demand volatility. They can pose challenges for inventory control, as demand can be difficult to predict. For BZ items, businesses must closely monitor market trends and adapt their strategies to accommodate short-term demand shifts. A more responsive supply chain may be needed to keep these items in stock during peak demand periods.

CX (Low Value, Stable Demand): Low-value items with stable demand are typically easier to manage, as they can be ordered in predictable quantities. These items generally do not require significant attention, and businesses can apply cost-efficient inventory management methods, such as bulk ordering or using simple reorder point systems.

CY (Low Value, Moderate Fluctuation in Demand): These items experience moderate demand fluctuations, requiring periodic reviews and adjustments to inventory levels. Although their value is low, businesses must monitor their consumption patterns to ensure that they are not overstocked during slower periods or understocked during demand spikes.

CZ (Low Value, Highly Variable Demand): Low-value items with unpredictable demand are the most difficult to manage. Their consumption is erratic, making it challenging to forecast their needs. These items may require the most attention when it comes to risk management, such as reducing order quantities or increasing the use of agile replenishment methods. Businesses can minimize carrying costs by holding minimal stock or relying on just-in-time systems.

The combined approach of ABC and XYZ analysis allows businesses to create a nuanced inventory management strategy that addresses both the value and demand variability of inventory items. By evaluating each item based on both its value and consumption patterns, organizations can allocate resources more effectively, improve forecasting accuracy, and minimize the risks associated with stockouts and overstocking.

For instance, an AX item (high value, stable demand) may be managed with a JIT inventory system, ensuring availability while minimizing storage costs. Meanwhile, a BZ item (moderate value, highly variable demand) may require the business to develop a more flexible approach, utilizing safety stock, demand sensing, or expedited ordering to meet unpredictable demand spikes.

Conclusion

XYZ analysis provides valuable insights into the consumption patterns of inventory items, complementing the traditional ABC analysis that focuses on their value and importance. By combining the two approaches, businesses can develop a more sophisticated inventory management system that accounts for both the criticality of an item and the variability in its demand. This dual classification system enables organizations to prioritize inventory control efforts, optimize replenishment strategies, and mitigate risks associated with stockouts and overstocking. As demand patterns continue to evolve, the integration of ABC and XYZ analysis can serve as a strategic tool for businesses to stay agile, efficient, and competitive in today's dynamic supply chain environment.

Chapter 6: Pareto Principle in Inventory Management

In the world of inventory management, one of the key challenges organizations face is determining how to allocate resources most effectively while minimizing costs. The Pareto Principle, also known as the 80/20 rule, offers a powerful framework for addressing this issue. It posits that, in many scenarios, 80% of outcomes are driven by just 20% of inputs. In the context of inventory management, this translates to the idea that a small percentage of inventory items typically account for the majority of the value or demand within the system. By identifying these high-impact items and optimizing resources accordingly, businesses can significantly improve their inventory efficiency and reduce costs.

Identifying High-Impact Inventory Items

One of the primary applications of the Pareto Principle in inventory management is identifying the small number of inventory items that drive the majority of the value, sales, or operational impact. Often, a minority of items represent the bulk of a company's revenue or consumption, and as such, these items demand special attention in terms of stock levels, ordering frequency, and management practices. Recognizing these high-impact items allows businesses to prioritize their resources and focus efforts on areas that have the greatest potential for improving efficiency.

To apply the Pareto Principle in inventory management, companies typically conduct an analysis that ranks inventory items by their sales, revenue contribution, or usage. This is known as a **Pareto analysis** or **80/20 analysis**, where the 20% of items with the highest sales or demand are identified. These items represent the high-impact portion of the inventory that should be prioritized.

In practice, inventory items are often categorized into three groups:

A Items: These are the top 20% of items that contribute to 80% of sales, revenue, or usage. A-items are considered critical, and they often account for the largest portion of working capital invested in inventory. Businesses must prioritize these items by ensuring they are consistently available, closely monitoring demand, and applying efficient inventory management practices like just-in-time (JIT) or automated replenishment systems to minimize stockouts or excess inventory.

B Items: The next tier, B-items, might represent about 30% of the inventory and contribute to around 15% of sales or demand. While B-items are not as critical as A-items, they still have a meaningful impact on overall performance. These items should be managed with less frequency and flexibility, such as implementing safety stock policies and setting reorder points, ensuring that stock levels are maintained without overburdening the inventory system.

C Items: C-items are the remaining 50% of the inventory, typically accounting for only 5% of the sales or usage. These items may not contribute significantly to the overall operations but are still necessary for business continuity. C-items often include low-value or low-demand products that can be stocked in bulk or less frequently restocked. For C-items, businesses can use simpler inventory management strategies like periodic ordering or batch replenishment, as these items have a relatively low impact on cash flow or overall operational efficiency.

The key to applying the Pareto Principle effectively in inventory management is recognizing that not all items require the same level of attention or resources. By focusing efforts on the high-impact items (A-items) and streamlining the management of lower-impact items (B- and C-items), businesses can allocate resources more efficiently and maintain the appropriate stock levels across the entire inventory.

Optimizing Resources for Maximum Efficiency

Once high-impact inventory items have been identified through Pareto analysis, businesses can optimize their resources for maximum efficiency by aligning their inventory practices with the demands of A-, B-, and C-items. Different items require different approaches to inventory management, and applying the right strategy to each category can significantly reduce waste, lower costs, and improve operational performance.

For **A-items**, which are high-value or high-demand items, businesses should prioritize inventory strategies that ensure availability without overstocking. For example, advanced demand forecasting methods, automated inventory systems, and just-in-time inventory practices can be employed for A-items to ensure that stock levels are closely aligned with actual demand, reducing the risks of stockouts and excess inventory. In many cases, A-items may require frequent reordering and close monitoring of sales trends to anticipate fluctuations in demand.

For **B-items**, which represent a moderate impact, businesses should aim for a balanced approach. These items are important but not as critical as A-items, so they require a less intense level of monitoring. However, inventory strategies such as setting reorder points, utilizing safety stock, and adopting periodic review systems are effective ways to manage B-items. The focus for B-items should be on maintaining an optimal stock level that accounts for variations in demand without overcommitting resources.

For **C-items**, which have a low impact on the overall business, businesses can adopt more straightforward and resource-efficient inventory management strategies. C-items may be ordered in bulk to minimize ordering costs, and replenishment may occur on a less frequent basis. In some cases, it may be beneficial to apply an **economic order quantity (EOQ)** model to minimize ordering and holding costs, ensuring that the business does not waste valuable resources on items that have a minimal impact on overall profitability.

The Pareto Principle also supports the idea of **inventory segmentation**, where resources are allocated differently based on the importance of the inventory category. For example, A-items may require dedicated personnel or advanced forecasting models to manage effectively, while B- and C-items may be handled by less specialized staff or automated inventory systems that are less resource-intensive.

Optimizing Supplier Relationships

In addition to optimizing internal resources, the Pareto Principle can be applied to **supplier management**. A-businesses often rely on a select group of key suppliers for their critical items, and these suppliers should be treated as strategic partners. Building strong relationships with these suppliers, negotiating favorable terms, and ensuring reliable delivery schedules can help secure the timely replenishment of A-items.

For B- and C-items, businesses may have more flexibility in their supplier relationships, as these items are less critical. In these cases, businesses may be able to work with a broader set of suppliers or rely on less frequent orders, reducing the administrative and logistical burden associated with these items. In some cases, consolidating suppliers for non-critical items can lead to economies of scale, reducing overall procurement costs.

Utilizing Technology to Improve Efficiency

Technology plays an increasingly important role in inventory optimization and the application of the Pareto Principle. Automated inventory management systems, demand forecasting software, and advanced data analytics tools can all help businesses apply Pareto analysis more effectively. These technologies can provide real-time data on inventory levels, sales patterns, and customer preferences, allowing businesses to make data-driven decisions about stock levels, ordering cycles, and replenishment strategies.

For A-items, advanced demand forecasting models can be used to predict fluctuations in demand with greater accuracy, helping businesses avoid stockouts and reduce excess inventory. For B- and C-items, automated reorder systems can help ensure that inventory levels remain balanced without the need for manual intervention. By integrating technology into the inventory management process, businesses can ensure that they are applying the Pareto Principle efficiently and achieving maximum efficiency across their entire inventory system.

Conclusion

The Pareto Principle is a powerful tool in inventory management, providing businesses with a framework for prioritizing resources and optimizing stock levels. By identifying the high-impact items in their inventory and applying differentiated management strategies, companies can maximize efficiency, minimize costs, and improve their overall operational performance. With the help of technology and strategic supplier relationships, businesses can further enhance the impact of Pareto analysis and drive improvements across all inventory categories. Ultimately, the Pareto Principle helps organizations achieve a more streamlined, efficient inventory management system that supports profitability and operational success.

Chapter 7: Advanced Inventory Categorization Methods

Effective inventory categorization is crucial for optimizing the management of stock levels, improving operational efficiency, and minimizing costs. Traditional methods such as **ABC** and **XYZ** analysis have been widely used in inventory management, providing valuable insights into the classification of inventory items based on their importance or demand patterns. However, as supply chains become more complex and dynamic, businesses are increasingly turning to **advanced inventory categorization methods** that offer more nuanced approaches to inventory classification. These methods go beyond the basic ABC and XYZ techniques and allow for deeper insights into inventory behavior, providing companies with a more comprehensive strategy for managing their inventory.

This chapter explores advanced inventory categorization methods, moving beyond the traditional ABC and XYZ models, and discusses their practical implementation in modern inventory management.

Methods Beyond ABC and XYZ

The ABC and XYZ analyses have been instrumental in inventory management for years, with ABC focusing on the value of inventory and XYZ focusing on demand variability. However, these models do not always capture the full spectrum of inventory behaviors or fully address the intricacies of modern supply chain operations. Advanced categorization methods incorporate multiple dimensions of inventory management, such as lifecycle, supply risk, and demand volatility, offering a more comprehensive approach.

1. VED Analysis (Vital, Essential, Desirable)

The **VED analysis** categorizes inventory based on its criticality to the business, differentiating between items that are essential for production or service delivery and those that are desirable but not critical. This method is particularly useful in industries where certain components or materials are vital for the smooth functioning of operations, while others may only be required intermittently or for non-core functions.

> **Vital (V):** Items in this category are absolutely essential for the company's operations. If these items are out of stock, it will result in a halt to production or service delivery. For example, in the healthcare industry, life-saving drugs or critical medical equipment would be considered vital.
>
> **Essential (E):** Items in this group are important for operations but may not be as critical as vital items. A temporary shortage of essential items might cause some operational delays or inefficiencies but will not completely halt production. For example, packaging materials or office supplies might fall into this category.
>
> **Desirable (D):** These items are not essential for immediate operations. While they may be necessary for customer satisfaction or to enhance the quality of the product or service, their absence will not severely disrupt operations. For instance, a marketing team's promotional materials might be categorized as desirable.

VED analysis helps organizations focus on securing vital and essential items, ensuring their supply is uninterrupted, while allowing for more flexibility in managing desirable items. This method complements traditional categorization models, especially in industries like healthcare, manufacturing, and technology, where the criticality of inventory can vary significantly.

2. FSN Analysis (Fast-moving, Slow-moving, Non-moving)

The **FSN analysis** classifies inventory based on its movement or sales frequency, providing businesses with insights into the flow of goods. Unlike ABC analysis, which is based on value or cost, FSN categorizes items based on how often they are used or sold. This method is particularly beneficial in industries with diverse product ranges or when businesses need to optimize storage space and working capital.

>**Fast-moving (F):** These items are characterized by high sales or usage rates. They are often stocked in large quantities, ensuring that businesses can meet demand without delays. Efficient inventory management of fast-moving items ensures they are always available for immediate use or sale.
>
>**Slow-moving (S):** These items are used or sold infrequently. Slow-moving inventory items may take up valuable storage space, and businesses may incur higher holding costs. However, it's important to carefully manage these items to avoid stockouts or excessive overstocking, which could lead to obsolescence or wastage.
>
>**Non-moving (N):** These items are rarely or never sold or used. Non-moving inventory represents a significant opportunity cost for businesses, as it ties up capital and warehouse space without providing any value. Regularly reviewing non-moving inventory and liquidating or discontinuing such items can free up resources and reduce carrying costs.

FSN analysis allows businesses to focus on managing fast-moving items efficiently while devising strategies to clear slow- and non-moving inventory. By differentiating the items based on movement speed, businesses can optimize warehouse space and improve cash flow management.

3. ROL Analysis (Replenishment, Obsolescence, Lead Time)

The **ROL analysis** considers the replenishment speed, the risk of obsolescence, and lead times in categorizing inventory. This method is particularly effective for businesses dealing with fast-paced industries like electronics, fashion, or food products, where the risk of inventory becoming obsolete or out-of-date is high. By evaluating items in terms of how quickly they need to be replenished, their shelf life, and the time it takes to restock them, ROL analysis helps businesses minimize excess inventory and reduce the risk of obsolescence.

> **Replenishment (R):** Items that require frequent replenishment to meet demand and prevent stockouts fall under this category. Replenishment-focused inventory should be managed using just-in-time strategies or automated ordering systems to ensure that the supply chain remains efficient and responsive.
>
> **Obsolescence (O):** Items with high obsolescence risk are typically products with short shelf lives or those susceptible to technological advancements. These items must be closely monitored for expiry dates, market changes, and potential for becoming obsolete. For instance, fashion items or consumer electronics are often categorized in this way.
>
> **Lead Time (L):** Lead time-focused inventory consists of items with varying procurement or manufacturing lead times. For items that take longer to procure, businesses need to plan ahead, ensuring that their ordering practices align with the longer replenishment periods.

ROL analysis is highly effective in industries with fast product lifecycles or volatile markets. It allows businesses to balance demand with supply chain capabilities, ensuring that stock levels are aligned with customer expectations and minimizing waste or lost sales.

4. SDE Analysis (Scarcity, Dependency, Expiry)

The **SDE analysis** categorizes inventory based on factors such as the scarcity of supply, the dependency on specific suppliers, and product expiration. This analysis is particularly useful in industries that depend on specialized materials, suppliers, or products with expiration dates, such as pharmaceuticals or food.

> **Scarcity (S):** Items that are scarce or difficult to procure due to limited availability or market constraints. These items require special attention to ensure that they are stocked adequately to avoid shortages.
>
> **Dependency (D):** Items that are highly dependent on specific suppliers or vendors. Any disruption in the supply chain for these items could lead to operational inefficiencies or bottlenecks. Businesses need to establish strong relationships with these suppliers and ensure contingency plans are in place.
>
> **Expiry (E):** Items with expiration dates or limited shelf lives. Products in this category must be managed carefully to ensure they are used or sold before they expire. For instance, perishable goods in food or pharmaceuticals require regular stock reviews and first-in, first-out (FIFO) inventory management methods.

SDE analysis allows businesses to account for the risks related to supplier dependency and expiration, focusing resources on securing supply chains and minimizing waste from expired or deteriorating products.

Practical Implementation

Implementing advanced inventory categorization methods requires a methodical approach that incorporates both data analysis and strategic decision-making. Here are the key steps involved in effectively implementing these advanced categorization methods:

Data Collection and Analysis: Accurate data on inventory levels, sales velocity, product lifecycles, supplier performance, and demand trends is essential. Implementing technologies such as **Warehouse Management Systems (WMS)** and **Enterprise Resource Planning (ERP)** systems can provide real-time visibility and insights into inventory behaviors.

Inventory Segmentation: After gathering the data, segment the inventory using the appropriate categorization methods based on the business's unique needs. For instance, businesses in high-tech industries may place more emphasis on ROL or SDE analysis due to the high risk of obsolescence and dependency on specific suppliers.

Develop Targeted Strategies: Once inventory has been categorized, businesses can tailor inventory management strategies for each category. For example, fast-moving items may benefit from frequent stock reviews and automated replenishment systems, while non-moving items may require liquidation strategies.

Review and Adjust: Regular reviews of inventory categories and their management strategies are essential for staying aligned with changes in demand, supply chain dynamics, and market conditions. Continuous analysis and adjustments ensure that inventory management remains responsive and efficient.

By adopting these advanced categorization methods, businesses can optimize their inventory management processes, reduce costs, and improve overall operational efficiency. The result is a more agile and responsive supply chain that can better meet customer needs while minimizing excess stock and waste.

Part 3: Inventory Forecasting

Chapter 8: The Role of Demand Forecasting

Importance of Accurate Forecasts

Demand forecasting is a critical aspect of inventory management, playing a central role in ensuring that businesses maintain optimal inventory levels to meet customer demand while avoiding overstocking or stockouts. Accurate forecasts help organizations plan and prepare for future demand, providing a solid foundation for inventory optimization strategies. With the increasing complexity and volatility of global supply chains, the importance of demand forecasting has never been greater.

An accurate demand forecast enables companies to anticipate fluctuations in customer demand, market conditions, and economic trends, allowing them to adjust their inventory procurement, storage, and distribution strategies accordingly. When forecasts are accurate, businesses can avoid common inventory-related challenges, such as excess inventory that ties up working capital or insufficient stock that leads to lost sales and customer dissatisfaction.

The role of demand forecasting extends beyond simple sales projections. It is integral to balancing supply and demand, reducing inventory holding costs, improving cash flow, and enhancing customer satisfaction. Accurate forecasts allow businesses to plan more effectively, ensuring that inventory is available when needed without incurring unnecessary costs. Furthermore, demand forecasting can help businesses make better-informed decisions related to procurement, production scheduling, and workforce planning, ultimately improving operational efficiency.

Aligning Forecasting with Inventory Goals

For demand forecasting to be truly effective, it must be closely aligned with the broader goals of inventory management. Inventory management aims to balance the need for sufficient stock to meet customer demand with the desire to minimize costs associated with inventory holding, ordering, and stockouts. A misalignment between forecasting and inventory goals can lead to inefficiencies and missed opportunities.

To ensure alignment, companies must integrate demand forecasting with their inventory management systems, creating a seamless flow of information that guides procurement, stocking, and replenishment decisions. Accurate demand forecasts inform key inventory strategies, including reorder points, safety stock levels, and order quantities. By adjusting these variables based on reliable forecasts, businesses can better manage their inventory levels, reduce waste, and minimize the risk of running out of stock.

Furthermore, aligning forecasting with inventory goals helps businesses tailor their strategies to different categories of inventory. For example, fast-moving items may require more frequent and precise forecasts to prevent stockouts, while slow-moving items may require less frequent forecasts to avoid excess stock. Accurate forecasting also enables businesses to identify seasonal trends and other demand fluctuations, allowing them to adjust inventory levels accordingly. By aligning demand forecasts with inventory objectives, businesses can implement targeted strategies for managing each inventory segment.

The accuracy of demand forecasting is influenced by several factors, including historical sales data, market trends, customer behavior, and external factors such as economic conditions or competitor actions. Leveraging advanced forecasting methods, such as time-series analysis, causal modeling, and machine learning algorithms, can significantly improve the accuracy of demand predictions. By using these tools, businesses can gain deeper insights into demand patterns and more effectively plan for future requirements.

In conclusion, demand forecasting plays an indispensable role in inventory management by ensuring that businesses have the right products available at the right time, in the right quantities. Accurate forecasts help align inventory strategies with organizational goals, ultimately leading to better resource utilization, reduced costs, and enhanced customer satisfaction. To remain competitive in today's fast-paced market, businesses must continuously refine their forecasting processes, integrating advanced analytical techniques and aligning them with their overall inventory management objectives. This proactive approach to demand forecasting is essential for maintaining operational efficiency and meeting customer expectations in an increasingly dynamic business environment.

Chapter 9: Forecasting Techniques

Qualitative vs. Quantitative Forecasting

Forecasting techniques are essential tools in inventory management, helping businesses predict future demand and adjust their inventory strategies accordingly. These techniques fall into two broad categories: qualitative and quantitative forecasting. Understanding the differences between these approaches and their respective advantages and limitations is crucial for selecting the right method for a given situation.

Qualitative Forecasting

Qualitative forecasting techniques rely on subjective judgment, intuition, and experience to make predictions about future demand. These methods are often used when there is little or no historical data available or when the data is too volatile to generate reliable quantitative forecasts. Qualitative forecasting is particularly useful in new product launches, market research, and situations where expert opinions or insights are more valuable than historical data.

Some common qualitative forecasting techniques include:

Expert Judgment: This method involves gathering input from industry experts, experienced employees, or stakeholders who have deep knowledge of the market, customer behavior, and the business environment. Their insights are used to predict future demand trends. This method is often subjective and may vary depending on the individual's perspective.

Market Research: Surveys, focus groups, and interviews with customers or potential buyers are used to gauge demand for a product. This approach can provide valuable qualitative data, particularly for new or niche products where there is limited historical data.

Delphi Method: This technique involves gathering opinions from a panel of experts through a series of questionnaires. The responses are aggregated and analyzed to generate a consensus forecast. This iterative process helps refine predictions by reducing biases and allowing for anonymous input.

Sales Force Opinion: Sales teams, who are in direct contact with customers, often have a good sense of demand trends. By collecting their forecasts, businesses can gain insights into customer preferences, potential changes in demand, and market conditions.

While qualitative methods are useful in certain situations, they can also be prone to bias and subjectivity. Therefore, they are typically used in conjunction with quantitative forecasting methods to provide a more balanced and comprehensive forecast.

Quantitative Forecasting

Quantitative forecasting techniques use historical data and statistical methods to make predictions about future demand. These methods are ideal for situations where historical data is available and the patterns of demand are relatively stable. Quantitative forecasting is more objective and based on measurable variables, making it highly suitable for businesses with large datasets and well-established product lines.

Common quantitative forecasting techniques include:

Time-Series Analysis: This is one of the most widely used methods for quantitative forecasting. Time-series analysis involves analyzing historical data to identify patterns and trends, such as seasonality, cyclic behavior, and long-term growth. By understanding these trends, businesses can predict future demand more accurately. Time-series analysis includes various techniques, such as moving averages, exponential smoothing, and trend analysis, to forecast demand based on past data.

Causal Models: These models use external variables, such as economic indicators, market conditions, or competitor actions, to predict future demand. By establishing relationships between demand and these influencing factors, businesses can make more informed forecasts. Regression analysis is a common technique used in causal modeling, where historical data is used to quantify the impact of independent variables on demand.

Simulation Models: Simulation involves creating a model of the demand process and running simulations to predict various outcomes based on different inputs. Monte Carlo simulation is one such method that uses random sampling to generate a range of possible demand scenarios, helping businesses prepare for uncertainty and variability in demand.

Quantitative forecasting techniques provide a more structured and data-driven approach to demand prediction. However, they also require large amounts of historical data and can be affected by changes in market conditions or unforeseen events that disrupt established patterns.

Time-Series Analysis and Seasonal Trends

Time-series analysis is a critical component of quantitative forecasting, particularly when dealing with demand patterns that repeat over time. Time-series data consists of a sequence of observations recorded at consistent intervals, such as daily, weekly, or monthly sales figures. By analyzing this data, businesses can identify trends, seasonal fluctuations, and other recurring patterns, which help refine future demand predictions.

Time-series analysis typically involves several key steps:

> **Trend Analysis**: A trend refers to the general direction in which demand is moving over time. It can be upward, downward, or flat. Identifying the trend helps businesses predict whether demand will continue to grow, decline, or remain stable in the future. Techniques like linear regression or moving averages can be used to identify trends in historical data.

> **Seasonality**: Many products experience seasonal fluctuations in demand, with certain periods of the year driving higher or lower sales. For example, winter coats typically see higher demand in colder months, while summer goods like beachwear and outdoor equipment may see a spike in demand during warmer months. Seasonality can be identified by analyzing historical

sales data and comparing the same periods in different years. Businesses can then adjust their inventory levels to account for these seasonal variations.

Cyclic Patterns: Unlike seasonal trends, which are regular and predictable, cyclic patterns refer to long-term fluctuations in demand that may be tied to broader economic cycles, such as periods of economic expansion or recession. Identifying cyclic patterns requires a more in-depth analysis of historical data and external factors, such as market conditions or industry performance.

Irregular or Random Fluctuations: Irregular fluctuations refer to unexpected changes in demand that are not part of regular trends or seasonal cycles. These can be caused by unforeseen events, such as natural disasters, strikes, or supply chain disruptions. While these fluctuations are difficult to predict, time-series analysis can help businesses identify periods of unusual activity and prepare contingency plans.

Time-series forecasting methods, such as moving averages and exponential smoothing, help smooth out irregular fluctuations and focus on the more predictable patterns in the data. Moving averages calculate the average demand over a set period, helping to filter out noise and highlight trends. Exponential smoothing assigns more weight to recent observations, making it more responsive to changes in demand. These methods allow businesses to generate forecasts that account for historical patterns while remaining flexible enough to adapt to changes in the market.

Incorporating Seasonal Trends into Forecasting

Seasonal trends are a critical component of time-series analysis, and understanding how to account for them is key to improving forecasting accuracy. Seasonal trends refer to fluctuations in demand that occur at regular intervals, often due to factors like weather, holidays, or cultural events. By analyzing historical sales data, businesses can identify seasonal patterns and adjust their forecasts accordingly.

For example, retailers can use seasonal forecasts to plan for demand spikes during holidays like Christmas or back-to-school seasons. Similarly, businesses in industries like agriculture or tourism can use seasonal trends to predict demand during peak growing seasons or vacation periods. By incorporating these trends into their forecasts, businesses can avoid overstocking or understocking inventory and ensure that they have the right products available at the right time.

Seasonal forecasting techniques, such as seasonal indices and decomposition methods, allow businesses to break down time-series data into its underlying components: trend, seasonality, and residual noise. This analysis helps isolate the effects of seasonal fluctuations and provides more accurate predictions for future demand.

Conclusion

Forecasting is a vital tool in inventory management, allowing businesses to predict demand and align inventory levels with future needs. Both qualitative and quantitative forecasting methods have their strengths and weaknesses, and businesses should select the most appropriate technique based on the availability of data, the complexity of demand patterns, and the level of uncertainty involved.

Time-series analysis, with its focus on identifying trends, seasonal patterns, and cyclic behavior, plays a central role in demand forecasting. By incorporating seasonal trends and adjusting forecasts to account for demand fluctuations, businesses can optimize inventory levels, reduce costs, and enhance customer satisfaction. Ultimately, effective forecasting enables businesses to stay ahead of the curve, make informed decisions, and maintain a competitive edge in

Chapter 10: Tools and Software for Inventory Forecasting

Overview of Leading Solutions

Effective inventory forecasting is an essential component of successful supply chain management, and the right tools and software can significantly enhance forecasting accuracy, efficiency, and decision-making. With the increasing complexity of global supply chains and the growing need for real-time data, businesses require advanced solutions that provide robust forecasting capabilities. Today, various inventory forecasting tools and software cater to a wide range of industries, helping companies streamline their inventory management processes, reduce stockouts and overstocking, and ultimately improve customer satisfaction and profitability.

Inventory forecasting software leverages historical data, advanced algorithms, and statistical models to predict future demand based on trends, seasonal variations, market conditions, and other factors. These tools offer a wide range of functionalities, from basic demand planning to sophisticated machine learning-powered predictions. Some solutions are standalone, while others are integrated with broader enterprise resource planning (ERP) or supply chain management systems. Selecting the right inventory forecasting tool depends on the specific needs of the business, the complexity of the inventory system, and the available resources.

Among the leading inventory forecasting software solutions are solutions from companies such as SAP, Oracle, NetSuite, and more specialized vendors like Forecast Pro and RELEX Solutions. These software platforms are designed to offer a variety of features aimed at improving the accuracy and effectiveness of inventory management.

SAP Integrated Business Planning (IBP) is one of the most prominent solutions in the market. It provides a comprehensive suite of tools for demand planning, inventory optimization, and supply chain management. The platform uses advanced analytics and machine learning models to generate forecasts and align inventory levels with future demand. SAP IBP integrates seamlessly with other SAP ERP systems, allowing businesses to synchronize inventory management with broader supply chain operations. With capabilities for collaborative planning, visibility, and real-time analytics, SAP IBP enables organizations to respond quickly to changing market conditions, helping to improve forecasting accuracy and optimize inventory levels.

Oracle's Demantra is another powerful forecasting solution, designed for companies looking for advanced demand forecasting and inventory optimization capabilities. Oracle Demantra offers a robust set of tools for demand sensing, statistical forecasting, and collaborative planning. The software can integrate with other Oracle supply chain management solutions, providing a unified platform for inventory management, demand planning, and sales forecasting. Oracle Demantra uses sophisticated algorithms to analyze historical data, identify demand patterns, and generate accurate forecasts. The software is highly customizable, enabling businesses to tailor forecasting models to their specific industry needs.

NetSuite, a cloud-based ERP platform, also provides inventory forecasting and demand planning capabilities. NetSuite's SuiteAnalytics Business Intelligence tool integrates with its inventory management system to provide insights into past demand patterns and forecast future requirements. The software offers real-time reporting and dashboards, allowing companies to monitor inventory levels and forecast demand more accurately. NetSuite's cloud-based nature also ensures that businesses can access their inventory data and forecasting tools from anywhere, improving collaboration and decision-making.

Specialized inventory forecasting solutions like Forecast Pro and RELEX Solutions offer deep functionality in the area of demand planning and inventory optimization. Forecast Pro is a widely used tool known for its easy-to-use interface and powerful statistical forecasting models. It offers features like automatic trend analysis, error tracking, and multi-level forecasting, making it a popular choice for businesses seeking a dedicated forecasting solution. RELEX Solutions, on the other hand, is a comprehensive supply chain optimization platform that includes forecasting, replenishment, and demand planning features. The software leverages artificial intelligence and machine learning to predict demand and optimize inventory levels across the supply chain. RELEX Solutions is particularly strong in industries like retail, where demand variability is high, and accurate forecasting is critical for maintaining optimal inventory levels.

Each of these tools has its strengths and weaknesses, and the right solution depends on factors such as company size, industry, available data, and specific forecasting requirements. Some businesses may opt for ERP-integrated solutions like SAP or Oracle, while others may prefer more specialized forecasting tools like Forecast Pro or RELEX Solutions. The key is selecting a tool that aligns with the organization's strategic goals and integrates seamlessly with existing supply chain management systems.

Implementation Best Practices

While the selection of the right forecasting tool is important, effective implementation is just as critical to achieving the desired outcomes. Implementing inventory forecasting software involves more than simply installing the tool and running it—successful implementation requires careful planning, clear communication, and ongoing optimization.

One of the first steps in implementing inventory forecasting software is aligning it with the organization's inventory management goals. This means clearly defining the objectives of the forecasting initiative, such as reducing stockouts, minimizing overstocking, improving service levels, or enhancing demand accuracy. Understanding these goals is essential for configuring the software and tailoring its features to meet specific business needs.

Once the goals are defined, it is important to gather the necessary data for accurate forecasting. Inventory forecasting relies heavily on historical sales data, demand patterns, and other key metrics, such as seasonality and lead times. Ensuring that the data is clean, accurate, and up-to-date is a fundamental part of the implementation process. Inaccurate or incomplete data will lead to flawed forecasts and poor decision-making. Businesses should also ensure that the data is integrated with other relevant systems, such as ERP or point-of-sale systems, to provide a complete view of inventory levels and demand trends.

After gathering the necessary data, the next step is configuring the software to suit the business's forecasting needs. Most inventory forecasting tools offer a range of customization options, allowing users to define the forecasting horizon, select the appropriate statistical models, and configure settings for demand seasonality, lead times, and safety stock levels. It is important to work with the software vendor or a consultant to ensure that the system is set up properly. This may involve selecting the right forecasting methods, customizing algorithms, and setting up reporting and dashboards to monitor forecast accuracy and performance.

Employee training is another crucial element in the successful implementation of inventory forecasting software. Even the most advanced tool will fail to deliver the expected results if the users do not know how to operate it effectively. Staff involved in inventory management, supply chain planning, and procurement should be thoroughly trained in how to use the software, interpret its outputs, and adjust forecasts as needed. Training should also cover how to troubleshoot common issues, adjust for changes in market conditions, and maintain data accuracy over time.

In addition to training, it is essential to establish a clear process for managing and updating forecasts. Forecasting is not a one-time activity but an ongoing process that requires continuous monitoring and refinement. As new data becomes available, businesses should adjust their forecasts accordingly. Regular reviews of forecast accuracy are essential to identify any discrepancies between predicted and actual demand and make adjustments as necessary. Many forecasting software solutions provide tools to measure forecast accuracy, such as mean absolute percentage error (MAPE), and offer features for improving forecast models based on historical performance.

Another best practice for implementing inventory forecasting software is ensuring cross-functional collaboration between different departments within the organization. Inventory forecasting does not happen in isolation; it requires input from sales, marketing, procurement, production, and finance teams. By collaborating and sharing information, businesses can generate more accurate forecasts that reflect real-world conditions. For example, marketing campaigns, new product launches, and promotional activities can significantly impact demand. Sales and marketing teams should work closely with supply chain planners to ensure that these factors are taken into account when generating forecasts.

Finally, it is important to continuously evaluate and optimize the forecasting process. This involves monitoring key performance indicators (KPIs) such as forecast accuracy, inventory turnover, stockouts, and customer service levels. By regularly assessing these metrics, businesses can identify areas for improvement and refine their forecasting models over time. Many forecasting software solutions include built-in analytics and reporting features that make it easier to track performance and identify trends. Additionally, as market conditions evolve and new technologies emerge, businesses should remain flexible and adapt their forecasting strategies to stay competitive.

In conclusion, implementing inventory forecasting software involves a combination of selecting the right tool, configuring it to meet the business's needs, training staff, and continuously optimizing the forecasting process. By aligning the tool with the organization's inventory management goals, gathering accurate data, and fostering collaboration across departments, businesses can significantly improve forecasting accuracy and efficiency. The right software, when used effectively, provides valuable insights into future demand, enabling businesses to optimize inventory levels, reduce costs, and enhance customer satisfaction.

Part 4: Inventory Control Systems

Chapter 11: Push and Pull Inventory Systems

Strengths and Weaknesses of Each Approach

In inventory management, two primary systems are commonly used to control and manage stock levels: push and pull inventory systems. Both systems have their unique advantages and disadvantages, and choosing the right one depends on several factors, including the nature of the business, demand patterns, production processes, and supply chain characteristics. Understanding the strengths and weaknesses of both push and pull systems is critical for organizations looking to optimize inventory control and improve overall supply chain efficiency.

Push Inventory System

The push inventory system is based on a forecast-driven approach. In this system, inventory is produced or ordered in advance based on anticipated demand, which is forecasted using historical data, market trends, or other predictive models. The production or procurement of goods is initiated regardless of whether actual demand materializes. Essentially, products are "pushed" through the supply chain based on predictions about future needs.

Strengths of Push Inventory System

Economies of Scale: Since products are manufactured or procured in bulk based on forecasts, organizations can take advantage of economies of scale. Bulk purchasing or large production runs often lead to cost savings per unit, making the push system an attractive option for businesses aiming to reduce unit costs.

Consistent Product Availability: By maintaining a consistent supply of inventory based on forecasts, businesses can reduce the likelihood of stockouts and ensure that products are available when customers need them. This is especially beneficial in industries where demand patterns are relatively stable and predictable.

Efficient Production Scheduling: The push system allows businesses to plan production schedules well in advance. Manufacturing processes can be optimized, and resources such as labor and equipment can be allocated efficiently. This is particularly beneficial for manufacturers with long lead times or complex production processes.

Supplier Relationships: The push system can foster strong relationships with suppliers, as they often work closely with businesses to fulfill long-term forecasts and production schedules. This can lead to improved reliability and better coordination throughout the supply chain.

Weaknesses of Push Inventory System

Risk of Overstocking: One of the most significant drawbacks of the push system is the risk of overstocking. Since inventory is produced based on forecasts, businesses may end up with excess stock if demand does not align with predictions. Overstocking can tie up valuable capital, increase storage costs, and lead to obsolete inventory, especially in industries with rapidly changing products.

Inflexibility: The push system can be rigid and slow to adapt to changes in market conditions or customer preferences. If demand shifts unexpectedly or new trends emerge, businesses may struggle to adjust their inventory levels quickly, resulting in stockouts or excess inventory.

Forecasting Errors: The push system relies heavily on accurate demand forecasting. If forecasts are inaccurate, businesses may face significant challenges, such as inventory shortages or surpluses. Overly optimistic forecasts can lead to the overproduction of products, while overly conservative forecasts can result in stockouts and missed sales opportunities.

Inventory Costs: Since the push system often involves maintaining larger quantities of inventory to meet forecasted demand, businesses may incur higher holding costs. These costs include warehousing, insurance, and the risk of inventory becoming obsolete. This is especially problematic in industries where products have short shelf lives or are subject to technological advancements.

Pull Inventory System

The pull inventory system, in contrast to the push system, is demand-driven. In a pull system, inventory is only ordered or produced when there is a customer demand for it. The production or replenishment process is triggered by actual consumption, rather than forecasts or predictions. This system is often associated with just-in-time (JIT) manufacturing, where the goal is to minimize inventory levels and eliminate waste.

Strengths of Pull Inventory System

Reduced Risk of Overstocking: One of the main benefits of the pull system is that it minimizes the risk of overstocking. Since inventory is replenished based on actual demand, businesses only produce or order what is needed, reducing the likelihood of excess stock and the associated costs.

Lower Inventory Costs: By maintaining lower inventory levels, businesses can significantly reduce inventory holding costs. The pull system encourages lean inventory practices, where inventory is replenished only when required, leading to more efficient use of storage space and reducing the financial burden of holding large quantities of stock.

Greater Flexibility: The pull system allows businesses to be more flexible and responsive to changes in customer demand. Since inventory is replenished based on actual consumption, companies can quickly adapt to shifts in market conditions, product preferences, or demand fluctuations without being burdened by excess inventory.

Improved Cash Flow: Since the pull system minimizes the need to carry large amounts of inventory, businesses can improve cash flow by reducing capital tied up in stock. The funds that would otherwise be spent on purchasing and storing excess inventory can be reinvested elsewhere in the business.

Weaknesses of Pull Inventory System

Risk of Stockouts: While the pull system reduces the risk of overstocking, it also increases the likelihood of stockouts. Since inventory is only replenished when there is demand, businesses may run out of stock if there are sudden spikes in demand or if there are delays in the production or supply chain. This can lead to lost sales, missed opportunities, and customer dissatisfaction.

Supply Chain Complexity: The pull system requires a high level of coordination and communication between various stakeholders in the supply chain. Since inventory is replenished based on actual demand, companies must ensure that suppliers, manufacturers, and distributors are all able to respond quickly to changes in demand. This can increase the complexity of supply chain operations and require sophisticated systems for real-time inventory tracking and demand forecasting.

Production and Lead Time Challenges: The pull system relies on the ability to produce or replenish inventory quickly in response to demand. However, in some industries, production lead times can be long, and supply chain disruptions can delay the delivery of goods. If a business experiences delays in production or supplier lead times, it may struggle to meet customer demand, especially for time-sensitive products.

High Dependence on Accurate Demand Data: Like the push system, the pull system also requires accurate data, but in this case, the system relies on real-time information regarding customer demand. If the data is inaccurate or outdated, it can lead to stockouts, delays, or mismatches between supply and demand.

When to Use Push or Pull

Deciding when to use a push or pull inventory system depends on several factors, including the type of business, the predictability of demand, production lead times, and the cost structure of the supply chain.

The push system is best suited for businesses that deal with relatively stable demand patterns and products that have long shelf lives or slow production cycles. Industries such as manufacturing, wholesale distribution, and consumer goods often benefit from the push system, as they can produce in bulk and take advantage of economies of scale. The push system is also appropriate when businesses need to ensure product availability, maintain high service levels, or when dealing with high-volume, low-margin products.

On the other hand, the pull system is ideal for businesses that operate in industries with unpredictable demand, fast-moving products, or where inventory costs are high. The pull system is often used in just-in-time (JIT) manufacturing, where minimizing inventory and reducing waste are critical to the business model. Industries such as automotive, electronics, and high-fashion retail often rely on the pull system to maintain lean inventory levels and respond quickly to changing customer preferences.

In many cases, businesses may adopt a hybrid approach that combines elements of both push and pull systems. For instance, a company may use a push system to produce goods based on forecasted demand for a product line, but implement a pull system for replenishing inventory at the retail level, based on actual sales. This hybrid approach allows businesses to strike a balance between maintaining product availability and reducing the risk of overstocking.

In conclusion, both push and pull inventory systems offer unique strengths and weaknesses, and the best choice depends on the specific needs of the business. By understanding the key characteristics of each system and evaluating factors such as demand variability, production lead times, and supply chain complexity, businesses can make informed decisions about which approach to adopt for optimal inventory control.

Chapter 12: Reorder Systems for Inventory Control

Fixed Order Quantity System

The **Fixed Order Quantity System** is one of the most widely used reorder systems in inventory management. Under this system, a fixed quantity of inventory is ordered each time the stock level reaches a predetermined reorder point. The quantity ordered is constant, regardless of the time elapsed since the last order or fluctuations in demand. This method is particularly useful when managing high-demand, standardized products where usage is relatively predictable and consistent.

A key feature of the Fixed Order Quantity System is that it provides a straightforward approach to managing inventory levels. By ordering a fixed quantity, businesses can ensure they maintain a consistent inventory flow, preventing stockouts while minimizing the need to monitor inventory levels constantly. However, this system can lead to either excess inventory or insufficient stock if demand varies significantly from what was expected, making forecasting accuracy crucial.

Fixed Periodic Review System

The **Fixed Periodic Review System** differs from the Fixed Order Quantity System in that inventory is checked at regular intervals (e.g., weekly, monthly) rather than constantly monitored. During each review period, a decision is made about how much to order based on the current stock level and the predetermined target inventory level. The order is made so that after the order is received, the inventory will return to the desired level.

This system is advantageous for businesses with fluctuating demand or those that want to avoid frequent ordering, as the review occurs at set times, making it easier to manage inventory and plan purchasing. However, one of the challenges with this system is that the amount ordered can vary significantly from one period to another, especially if demand fluctuates widely between review periods. This makes it harder to maintain a consistent inventory level and may result in stockouts or overstocking.

Two-Bin and Three-Bin Systems

The **Two-Bin System** is a simple and effective method for controlling inventory, particularly in environments where stockouts can be critical. Under this system, inventory is divided into two bins: one bin is used for active inventory, while the second bin is a backup. When the first bin runs out of stock, an order is placed to replenish it. This ensures that there is always a buffer in place, minimizing the risk of running out of inventory.

The **Three-Bin System** is an extension of the two-bin system. In this approach, there are three bins: the first is used for active inventory, the second serves as a backup, and the third is a reserve or safety stock. The third bin acts as an extra cushion for high-demand items or during uncertain times. This system further reduces the likelihood of stockouts by providing additional layers of protection. However, the challenge with both the two-bin and three-bin systems is the need for more physical space to store the extra bins, which can increase storage costs.

Min-Max Inventory Control System

The **Min-Max Inventory Control System** is a commonly used approach for managing inventory levels. It involves setting a minimum inventory level (the reorder point) and a maximum inventory level. When the inventory reaches the minimum level, an order is placed to replenish it, bringing the stock up to the maximum level. This system provides a balance between maintaining enough inventory to meet demand and preventing excess stock, which can tie up capital and increase holding costs.

The Min-Max system is simple to implement and effective for businesses that deal with a variety of products with different demand patterns. However, the main drawback is that it requires constant monitoring of inventory levels to ensure that orders are placed when stock reaches the reorder point. Additionally, if demand is unpredictable, the system may result in stockouts or overstocking if the minimum and maximum levels are not set correctly.

Kanban-Based Reorder Systems

The **Kanban-Based Reorder System** is a visual inventory control system that uses cards or signals (kanban cards) to trigger the replenishment process. Each card corresponds to a specific quantity of inventory, and when the stock reaches a certain threshold, the card is moved to signal the need for a reorder. This system is commonly used in just-in-time (JIT) manufacturing environments, where minimizing inventory levels and ensuring a smooth flow of materials are key priorities.

The strength of the Kanban system lies in its simplicity and ability to synchronize production and inventory levels with actual demand. As inventory levels fluctuate, kanban cards ensure that new orders are placed only when necessary, helping to prevent both stockouts and overstocking. However, this system requires a well-organized system of tracking and managing kanban cards, which can be a challenge in complex supply chains or for businesses with a large number of products.

Economic Order Quantity (EOQ) Reorder Systems

The **Economic Order Quantity (EOQ)** system is a mathematical model used to determine the optimal order quantity that minimizes the total cost of inventory, including ordering costs and holding costs. The EOQ formula helps businesses calculate the most cost-effective order quantity based on factors such as demand, ordering costs, and holding costs. By ordering the optimal quantity, businesses can reduce overall inventory costs and maintain efficient stock levels.

The EOQ system is highly effective for companies with relatively stable demand and predictable ordering costs. It provides a balanced approach to inventory control by minimizing the trade-off between ordering frequently in small quantities (which increases ordering costs) and ordering in large quantities (which increases holding costs). However, the EOQ model assumes a stable demand and ordering environment, making it less effective for businesses with significant demand variability or frequent changes in supply chain conditions.

Automated Reorder Systems

Automated Reorder Systems use technology to streamline the reorder process by automatically generating purchase orders based on predefined inventory levels and reorder points. These systems integrate with enterprise resource planning (ERP) systems, inventory management software, and barcode scanning technology to monitor inventory levels in real-time and trigger orders when necessary. Automated reorder systems can significantly reduce the administrative burden of manual inventory checks and orders, improving efficiency and reducing the risk of human error.

One of the main advantages of automated reorder systems is their ability to monitor inventory continuously and place orders without manual intervention. This is particularly beneficial for businesses with large inventories or those operating in fast-paced industries. By automating the process, companies can also improve inventory accuracy, minimize stockouts, and ensure that inventory levels remain optimal. However, automated systems require a significant upfront investment in technology and infrastructure, and they may require ongoing maintenance to ensure the system operates correctly.

Consignment and Vendor-Managed Inventory (VMI) Systems

Consignment and Vendor-Managed Inventory (VMI) Systems are inventory management approaches where the supplier is responsible for managing inventory levels at the customer's location. In consignment inventory, the supplier retains ownership of the inventory until it is used or sold. In VMI systems, the supplier monitors the customer's inventory levels and takes responsibility for replenishment decisions. Both systems aim to reduce inventory costs for the customer while providing the supplier with greater control over stock levels.

Consignment and VMI systems offer several benefits, including reduced capital investment for the customer, improved stock availability, and better coordination between suppliers and customers. These systems can also lead to more accurate inventory replenishment since the supplier is closely involved in monitoring stock levels. However, they require strong collaboration between the customer and supplier and may not be suitable for all businesses, particularly those with complex or high-demand inventory.

In conclusion, there are various reorder systems available to help businesses control their inventory effectively. The right system depends on factors such as the nature of the products, demand patterns, supply chain complexity, and the level of automation and technology available. By selecting the appropriate reorder system, businesses can optimize inventory levels, reduce costs, and improve overall operational efficiency.

Chapter 13: Advanced Inventory Models

Economic Order Quantity (EOQ)

The **Economic Order Quantity (EOQ)** model is one of the most fundamental and widely used inventory optimization tools. It aims to determine the optimal order size that minimizes total inventory costs, which include both ordering and holding costs. The EOQ model is particularly effective in environments where demand is relatively stable and predictable, and it assumes that both the demand for products and the costs associated with ordering and holding inventory are known and constant.

The core idea behind EOQ is to strike a balance between ordering inventory too frequently (which incurs high ordering costs) and ordering in large quantities (which leads to high holding costs). The EOQ formula is derived by minimizing the total cost function, which combines the cost of ordering and the cost of holding inventory. The formula for EOQ is:

$$EOQ = \sqrt{\frac{2DS}{H}}$$

Where:

D is the demand rate (units per period),

S is the ordering cost per order,

H is the holding or carrying cost per unit per period.

The EOQ model is highly effective in stable environments but may require adjustments in situations where demand fluctuates significantly or when there are frequent changes in supply chain conditions. While EOQ helps minimize inventory-related costs, it is less useful in highly dynamic or volatile markets where demand is irregular and difficult to predict.

Lot Sizing Models

Lot sizing refers to the process of determining the optimal quantity of items to order or produce at one time. Lot sizing is a critical element in manufacturing and inventory management because it directly affects both production scheduling and inventory costs. Various models can be used to calculate optimal lot sizes, depending on factors such as demand patterns, setup costs, and inventory carrying costs.

Two of the most commonly used lot sizing models are the **Economic Production Quantity (EPQ)** model and the **Silver-Meal Heuristic**.

The **Economic Production Quantity (EPQ)** model is an extension of the EOQ model and is used when items are produced in-house rather than ordered. It takes into account the production rate and the consumption rate of items and is particularly useful in situations where products are manufactured in batches. The EPQ model aims to determine the optimal batch size that minimizes the total costs of production and inventory holding.

The **Silver-Meal Heuristic** is another approach to lot sizing that is particularly useful when demand is variable. This method calculates the optimal lot size by minimizing the total cost per unit of demand over a given time period. It balances the ordering and holding costs by taking into account the time horizon and varying demand. While the Silver-Meal method is effective in dynamic environments, it requires continuous review and updating of demand data to ensure optimal results.

Newsvendor Model for Perishables

The **Newsvendor Model** is a specialized inventory optimization model used to manage perishable goods, such as food, pharmaceuticals, and other items with limited shelf life. Unlike traditional inventory models, the Newsvendor Model deals with uncertain demand and perishable products, where inventory cannot be stored for an extended period without incurring losses due to spoilage or expiration.

The goal of the Newsvendor Model is to determine the optimal order quantity that minimizes the cost of understocking (or lost sales) and the cost of overstocking (or excess inventory that may expire). The model operates under a single period of time and assumes that demand is uncertain, typically modeled as a probability distribution. The key metric in this model is the **critical ratio**, which represents the probability that demand will not exceed the order quantity. The formula for the critical ratio is:

$$CR = \frac{Cu}{Cu + Co}$$

Where:

Cu is the cost of understocking (e.g., lost sales),

Co is the cost of overstocking (e.g., holding costs or spoilage).

By calculating the critical ratio, the business can determine the optimal order quantity that minimizes the combined costs of overstocking and understocking. The Newsvendor Model is particularly valuable for managing perishable inventory, where traditional models may not adequately address the risks of spoilage or expiration. However, its main limitation is that it applies to single-period inventories, making it less suitable for multi-period or long-term inventory planning.

Multi-Echelon Inventory Optimization

Multi-Echelon Inventory Optimization (MEIO) is a more complex and advanced model used to manage inventory across multiple levels or stages in a supply chain. In a multi-echelon system, inventory is held at various points in the supply chain, such as at manufacturing plants, warehouses, distribution centers, and retail stores. The challenge with multi-echelon inventory management is to determine the optimal inventory levels at each stage of the supply chain to minimize total costs while ensuring that products are available when and where they are needed.

MEIO seeks to optimize inventory at each echelon (or level) of the supply chain by considering not only the individual costs at each level but also the interdependencies between different stages. For instance, the decision to order raw materials at the production level will impact the amount of finished goods available at the distribution center and retail stores. The goal is to optimize inventory at all levels simultaneously, ensuring that each level is appropriately stocked without creating excess inventory at any stage of the supply chain.

One key challenge of MEIO is managing the trade-offs between holding costs at different levels of the supply chain. For example, holding inventory at the manufacturing level may lead to higher holding costs, but it can also reduce transportation costs by providing sufficient stock to meet demand at downstream locations. The **Bullwhip Effect**, where small fluctuations in demand at the retail level cause large fluctuations in inventory levels at upstream levels of the supply chain, is a significant issue in multi-echelon inventory systems. MEIO models aim to mitigate the Bullwhip Effect by improving demand forecasting, inventory replenishment strategies, and communication across the supply chain.

Conclusion

Advanced inventory models like the **Economic Order Quantity (EOQ), Lot Sizing Models, Newsvendor Model**, and **Multi-Echelon Inventory Optimization** provide businesses with powerful tools to manage inventory more efficiently. While each model has its strengths and is suited to specific inventory types and business environments, they all aim to balance costs and inventory availability. EOQ is highly effective for stable demand environments, while Lot Sizing Models and the Newsvendor Model are useful for managing production and perishable goods, respectively. Multi-Echelon Inventory Optimization addresses the complexities of modern, multi-level supply chains and helps mitigate challenges like the Bullwhip Effect. By leveraging these models, businesses can optimize inventory levels, reduce costs, and improve overall supply chain performance.

Part 5: Optimizing Stock Levels

Chapter 14: Safety Stock Management

Principles of Safety Stock

Safety stock plays a pivotal role in inventory management by acting as a buffer between supply and demand uncertainties. The fundamental principle behind safety stock is to ensure that businesses are prepared for fluctuations in demand or lead times, which can disrupt the normal flow of inventory. The purpose of safety stock is to mitigate the risk of stockouts, which could lead to lost sales, customer dissatisfaction, or production delays. It helps to provide a cushion when actual demand exceeds forecasted demand or when there are unforeseen delays in the supply chain.

In inventory management, safety stock is typically calculated based on variability in both demand and lead time. The more variable these two factors are, the higher the safety stock level required to maintain service levels. Safety stock serves as a protective measure against unexpected changes in demand, whether caused by seasonal shifts, market fluctuations, or sudden changes in customer behavior.

The calculation of safety stock often involves using statistical methods to measure demand variability and lead time variability. One common formula for calculating safety stock involves determining the standard deviation of demand during the lead time period. The greater the variation in demand, the higher the safety stock needed to maintain desired service levels. Another common approach is using a **service level** approach, where safety stock is calculated to achieve a target service level (the probability of not having a stockout during a specific period).

The goal of safety stock management is not to overstock, as this leads to excessive holding costs, nor is it to understock, which increases the likelihood of stockouts and missed sales opportunities. Instead, it involves finding the optimal level of safety stock that minimizes both risks and costs.

Balancing Risk and Cost

One of the key challenges in safety stock management is balancing the risks associated with stockouts against the costs of holding excess inventory. Stockouts can lead to lost sales, customer dissatisfaction, or production stoppages, which can damage a company's reputation and bottom line. On the other hand, carrying too much safety stock increases inventory holding costs, such as storage, insurance, and the opportunity cost of tied-up capital.

To achieve an optimal balance between risk and cost, businesses must carefully assess factors such as demand variability, lead time variability, and service level targets. High-demand variability or long lead times typically require higher safety stock levels to reduce the probability of stockouts. However, it is also essential to recognize the costs associated with carrying excess inventory, such as the cost of capital, storage, and obsolescence. Therefore, safety stock levels must be periodically reviewed and adjusted to reflect changes in demand patterns, lead times, and business objectives.

Several strategies can help businesses strike this balance:

> **Demand Forecasting and Lead Time Analysis**: Accurate demand forecasting and lead time analysis are critical for determining appropriate safety stock levels. By using advanced forecasting methods and tracking historical trends, businesses can reduce the uncertainty surrounding future demand and supply timelines, thereby minimizing the need for high safety stock levels. For example, businesses can use time-series analysis or machine learning models to predict demand more

accurately, reducing the chances of over- or understocking.

Service Level Targets: Setting clear service level targets is another key factor in balancing risk and cost. A business might aim for a 95% service level, meaning that there is a 95% chance that it will have the inventory on hand to meet customer demand. The higher the service level target, the more safety stock is required to buffer against demand and supply uncertainty. Companies must consider their specific market dynamics and customer expectations when determining their desired service level.

Inventory Replenishment Strategies: Using efficient inventory replenishment strategies, such as just-in-time (JIT) or vendor-managed inventory (VMI), can help minimize the need for large safety stock levels. These approaches focus on closely aligning inventory replenishment with actual demand, reducing the chances of both overstocking and stockouts. For example, in a JIT system, safety stock may be kept at minimal levels, relying on frequent and predictable deliveries from suppliers.

Periodic Reviews and Adjustments: Safety stock levels should not be static. They must be reviewed and adjusted regularly based on changes in demand, lead times, and other operational factors. By continuously monitoring inventory levels, lead times, and demand fluctuations, companies can optimize their safety stock levels and prevent unnecessary costs.

Advanced Inventory Management Systems: Modern inventory management systems, such as those powered by artificial intelligence (AI) and machine learning, can provide real-time insights into demand patterns, lead times, and inventory levels. These systems can help businesses make data-driven decisions on safety stock levels by integrating demand forecasting, lead time analysis, and inventory replenishment into a unified system. Furthermore, automated inventory systems can trigger alerts when safety stock levels approach critical thresholds, ensuring that timely action is taken to reorder stock before shortages occur.

Supplier Collaboration and Flexibility: Working closely with suppliers to improve lead times and demand forecasting can help reduce the need for large safety stocks. Supplier collaboration ensures that businesses can rely on timely deliveries and can better anticipate fluctuations in demand. In some cases, suppliers may offer flexibility, such as expedited shipping or the ability to increase production capacity during peak demand periods, further minimizing the need for high safety stock levels.

Multi-Sourcing and Buffer Strategies: In industries where supply chain disruptions are common, such as in global sourcing environments, businesses may opt for multi-sourcing strategies. This involves sourcing the same product from multiple suppliers, reducing the risk of relying on a single source and increasing flexibility in the supply chain. Buffer strategies, such as maintaining safety stock at various points in the supply chain (e.g., at the supplier, warehouse, and retail levels), can also provide additional layers of protection against stockouts.

The Trade-Off: Cost vs. Customer Satisfaction

Safety stock management ultimately comes down to a trade-off between cost and customer satisfaction. High safety stock levels reduce the risk of stockouts, ensuring that customers' needs are met and that production processes continue uninterrupted. However, this comes at a cost. Carrying excess inventory increases storage costs, ties up capital, and may result in product obsolescence, especially for perishable goods or products with limited shelf life. Excessive inventory also reduces inventory turnover, which can impact a company's profitability.

Conversely, having too little safety stock exposes the business to the risk of stockouts, lost sales, and dissatisfied customers. This risk is particularly critical in industries with high customer expectations for product availability, such as the retail or high-tech sectors. Stockouts can not only lead to immediate revenue loss but also damage long-term customer loyalty.

To strike the right balance, businesses must align their safety stock strategy with their overall inventory management objectives and customer satisfaction goals. For example, a business operating in a highly competitive retail market may prioritize customer satisfaction over cost savings and opt for higher safety stock levels to ensure it meets customer demand consistently. On the other hand, a company with a more niche product offering may choose to minimize safety stock to reduce holding costs and accept the risk of occasional stockouts, especially if demand is relatively predictable.

Conclusion

Safety stock management is a critical aspect of inventory optimization that helps businesses balance the risks of stockouts with the costs of holding excess inventory. By understanding the principles of safety stock and implementing strategies such as accurate demand forecasting, setting appropriate service level targets, and utilizing advanced inventory management systems, companies can achieve optimal safety stock levels that minimize both risk and cost. Effective safety stock management ensures that businesses can meet customer demand while maintaining efficient inventory practices, ultimately contributing to improved operational efficiency, customer satisfaction, and profitability.

Chapter 15: Inventory Rationalization Strategies

Assessing Inventory Across Multiple Locations

Inventory rationalization is a critical process that involves evaluating and optimizing inventory levels across various locations within a supply chain or business network. For companies that operate multiple warehouses, retail locations, or distribution centers, managing inventory effectively can be a challenge. A lack of centralized control and oversight can lead to inefficiencies, such as overstocking in one location while another faces stockouts. The goal of inventory rationalization is to streamline operations by assessing inventory levels, demand patterns, and storage capabilities across all locations to ensure that inventory is balanced and optimized.

The process begins by performing a comprehensive audit of the inventory at each location. This audit includes reviewing current stock levels, product turnover rates, and historical demand data. By analyzing the demand patterns for each product across locations, businesses can identify where inventory is underutilized or overstocked. Additionally, businesses must consider factors such as lead time, transportation costs, and seasonal variations that may impact inventory decisions at different locations.

One of the primary benefits of assessing inventory across multiple locations is the ability to identify opportunities for consolidation. For example, if two locations are carrying large quantities of the same product, but one location experiences consistent stockouts while the other has excess inventory, it may make sense to redistribute the stock. This process not only helps to minimize overstocking but also ensures that products are available where they are needed most. Furthermore, it improves customer satisfaction by reducing the risk of stockouts at key locations.

A key aspect of this assessment is the role of technology. Inventory management systems that provide real-time visibility across all locations are essential for effective decision-making. With integrated software solutions, businesses can gain insights into stock levels, order status, and sales data across their entire network, enabling informed decisions about inventory distribution and replenishment.

Consolidating and Standardizing Inventory

Consolidation and standardization of inventory are central strategies in inventory rationalization. Consolidating inventory involves reducing the total number of locations where inventory is held, either by merging warehouses, shifting stock from underperforming locations to high-demand ones, or eliminating redundant stock. The aim is to reduce complexity and improve inventory flow, which in turn reduces costs associated with carrying excess inventory.

Standardizing inventory refers to the process of unifying product offerings, SKU management, and stock-keeping practices across all locations. In many businesses, different locations may have variations in how inventory is labeled, categorized, or managed. This lack of standardization can lead to inefficiencies, confusion, and difficulty in tracking inventory accurately. By standardizing these processes, businesses can achieve more consistent inventory control and reporting, which helps streamline operations across locations.

Consolidation and standardization also simplify the replenishment process. With a standardized inventory system, companies can ensure that the same products are replenished consistently across locations, reducing the complexity involved in ordering and managing stock. This simplification also enables businesses to take advantage of bulk purchasing or centralized procurement, leading to cost savings on purchasing and storage.

For example, in retail, where businesses may have hundreds of stores, consolidating inventory allows for better tracking of fast-moving items and ensures that the right products are distributed to stores based on demand. In warehouses or distribution centers, this could mean optimizing the use of warehouse space by eliminating duplicate SKUs and consolidating them into fewer, larger locations, ultimately reducing handling and storage costs.

Benefits in Cost Savings and Efficiency

The primary goal of inventory rationalization is to improve efficiency while reducing costs. By assessing inventory across multiple locations and consolidating and standardizing stock, businesses can achieve significant cost savings. These savings arise from a variety of areas:

> **Reduction in Carrying Costs**: One of the most significant benefits of inventory rationalization is the reduction in inventory holding costs. By consolidating inventory across fewer locations, businesses can minimize the amount of stock they need to store, which reduces the cost of warehouse space, insurance, utilities, and other overheads. Lowering carrying costs allows businesses to free up capital that would otherwise be tied up in excess inventory.

> **Improved Inventory Turnover**: Rationalizing inventory ensures that products move more efficiently through the supply chain. By aligning stock levels with actual demand and minimizing overstocking, businesses can improve inventory turnover. Faster turnover means that inventory is being replenished at the right time, reducing the need for large safety stock reserves and helping businesses to manage working capital more effectively.

Decreased Stockouts and Overstocking: Inventory rationalization helps to optimize stock levels, reducing the risk of both stockouts and overstocking. By ensuring that inventory is balanced across multiple locations based on actual demand patterns, businesses can avoid situations where products are either sitting idle in warehouses or running out at the point of sale. This improves customer satisfaction, as customers are more likely to find the products they need when they need them, without delays.

Lower Transportation and Distribution Costs: By consolidating inventory into fewer locations, businesses can achieve better economies of scale in transportation and distribution. Instead of managing multiple smaller shipments to different locations, consolidated inventory can be distributed in larger, more cost-effective shipments. Additionally, having inventory centrally located allows for more efficient use of delivery routes, reducing fuel consumption and lowering overall transportation costs.

Reduced Complexity in Management: A more streamlined inventory system, with fewer locations and standardized processes, reduces the complexity of managing inventory. Fewer products to track and fewer locations to oversee make inventory management simpler and more efficient. This reduces the time spent on inventory counting, replenishment planning, and order fulfillment. As a result, the business can focus more on value-adding activities and improving customer service.

Enhanced Data Accuracy and Forecasting: Standardizing inventory practices and consolidating stock provides businesses with more accurate and reliable data. With fewer variables in the system, businesses can more easily track inventory movement and gain clearer insights into demand patterns. This allows for more accurate forecasting and better-informed purchasing decisions. With improved forecasting accuracy, businesses can optimize ordering cycles and avoid last-minute rush orders that lead to increased costs.

Better Supplier Relationships and Negotiations: Consolidating inventory and streamlining procurement processes can lead to stronger relationships with suppliers. Businesses with consolidated orders can negotiate better pricing and terms with suppliers, as they can purchase in larger volumes, resulting in discounts or improved lead times. Suppliers may also benefit from more predictable ordering patterns, which can lead to smoother supply chain operations.

Improved Customer Service: Rationalizing inventory ensures that the right products are available at the right locations to meet customer demand. By reducing stockouts and ensuring faster replenishment, businesses can offer a higher level of service to customers. Timely order fulfillment and product availability directly impact customer satisfaction and loyalty, which are essential for long-term success.

Conclusion

Inventory rationalization is a powerful strategy for businesses looking to reduce costs, increase efficiency, and improve service levels. By assessing inventory across multiple locations, consolidating stock, and standardizing inventory management practices, businesses can achieve significant cost savings and streamline their operations. The benefits of inventory rationalization go beyond just cost reduction; they also result in improved inventory turnover, lower transportation costs, better data accuracy, and ultimately, enhanced customer satisfaction. In today's competitive business environment, inventory rationalization is an essential tool for businesses aiming to optimize their supply chain and achieve operational excellence.

Part 6: Inventory Optimization Strategies

Chapter 16: Lean Inventory Management

Principles of Lean and Waste Reduction

Lean inventory management is a methodology that focuses on reducing waste and improving efficiency within the supply chain. It stems from the broader principles of Lean, a concept originally developed by Toyota to optimize production processes. The core goal of Lean is to maximize value by minimizing waste, often referred to as the "seven wastes" (Muda, Mura, and Muri). These include overproduction, waiting time, unnecessary transportation, over-processing, excess inventory, unnecessary movement, and defects.

When applied to inventory management, Lean principles seek to reduce or eliminate non-value-added activities in inventory handling and storage. This approach emphasizes that inventory should only be ordered and stored when it is needed, ensuring that resources are utilized optimally and that inventory levels align directly with demand. Through Lean techniques, businesses aim to enhance operational efficiency by reducing excess stock, improving inventory turnover, and decreasing carrying costs. By focusing on eliminating waste, Lean inventory management not only streamlines processes but also improves cash flow by reducing capital tied up in unsold goods.

One of the key concepts of Lean inventory management is Just-in-Time (JIT) inventory. This principle advocates for producing or ordering goods only when needed, rather than keeping large amounts of stock in hand. By aligning inventory levels with actual demand, businesses avoid overstocking and reduce the associated holding costs. Lean also emphasizes continuous improvement (Kaizen), where processes are constantly evaluated and refined to identify inefficiencies and bottlenecks. Through this iterative approach, Lean inventory management helps businesses stay agile and responsive to market changes.

Tools for Lean Inventory (5S, Value Stream Mapping, Kanban)

Lean inventory management relies on several tools and techniques to optimize processes and eliminate waste. These tools help businesses improve efficiency, streamline operations, and create a culture of continuous improvement. Some of the most widely used Lean tools in inventory management include 5S, Value Stream Mapping (VSM), and Kanban.

5S is a methodology that focuses on workplace organization and standardization to create a clean, efficient, and productive environment. The five steps in 5S are: Sort, Set in order, Shine, Standardize, and Sustain. In inventory management, this approach ensures that only necessary items are kept in the warehouse, that they are stored in an organized and easily accessible manner, and that workspaces are continuously maintained and improved. By creating an organized environment, businesses can reduce the time spent searching for items, reduce unnecessary movements, and improve safety and quality.

Value Stream Mapping (VSM) is a powerful tool used to analyze and visualize the flow of materials and information across a process or supply chain. In Lean inventory management, VSM helps identify inefficiencies, bottlenecks, and areas where waste occurs. By mapping out the entire process from supplier to customer, businesses can identify steps that add value and those that do not, allowing them to focus on streamlining operations. This helps to optimize inventory levels and reduce lead times by eliminating unnecessary processes and delays. The result is a more efficient, responsive supply chain with less inventory tied up in non-value-adding activities.

Kanban is a visual scheduling system that helps manage inventory and production in a Lean environment. Kanban uses cards, boards, or digital tools to signal the need for inventory replenishment or production. The system ensures that stock is ordered or produced only when necessary, preventing overproduction and minimizing excess inventory. Kanban systems typically involve two types of signals: one to indicate when a product or component is needed, and another to signal when inventory levels are replenished. Kanban can be implemented in various forms, such as a simple two-bin system or a more complex digital system that integrates with inventory management software. By providing clear visual signals, Kanban helps reduce stockouts and ensure that inventory levels are maintained at optimal levels.

These tools, when used in conjunction with Lean principles, allow businesses to streamline their inventory management processes, improve workflow, and enhance overall efficiency. By embracing these tools, companies can reduce waste, lower inventory carrying costs, and improve customer satisfaction by ensuring the right products are available at the right time.

Case Studies of Lean Success

Many businesses across various industries have successfully implemented Lean inventory management to streamline operations, reduce waste, and improve profitability. These case studies highlight the power of Lean techniques in transforming inventory management practices.

Case Study 1: Toyota

The automotive giant Toyota is often considered the pioneer of Lean principles, and its success in inventory management is a direct result of the Just-in-Time (JIT) approach. Toyota implemented JIT to reduce excess inventory and improve production efficiency by ordering and receiving parts only when they were needed in the assembly process. By aligning production schedules with actual demand, Toyota minimized stockpiles and reduced the need for large warehouses, which in turn lowered costs associated with inventory storage and handling.

Through JIT, Toyota created a responsive and flexible supply chain that could quickly adjust to changes in demand. The company's implementation of Kanban, a key Lean tool, allowed workers to signal when parts needed to be replenished, ensuring that the right amount of inventory was always on hand. As a result, Toyota was able to significantly reduce lead times, increase production efficiency, and maintain high levels of product quality—all while minimizing inventory costs. Toyota's success story serves as a benchmark for businesses looking to implement Lean principles in inventory management.

Case Study 2: Walmart

Walmart is another company that has effectively implemented Lean inventory practices to improve its supply chain and inventory management. Walmart's approach to inventory optimization focuses on maintaining low inventory levels while ensuring products are always available for customers. The company uses a combination of technologies, such as automated inventory tracking and real-time data sharing with suppliers, to align inventory levels with customer demand.

Walmart's retail operations leverage Lean principles such as Value Stream Mapping and 5S to optimize its inventory management processes. By regularly evaluating its supply chain and distribution networks, Walmart ensures that it operates with minimal waste. The company also employs JIT to manage its inventory and replenishment cycles, ensuring that products arrive in stores only when they are needed. Walmart's Lean inventory practices have enabled the company to maintain low operating costs, provide competitive prices to customers, and remain agile in responding to changing consumer preferences.

Case Study 3: Dell Computers

Dell is known for its direct-to-consumer model, which heavily relies on Lean inventory management. The company uses a build-to-order approach, where computers are assembled based on customer orders rather than maintaining a large inventory of finished products. This approach allows Dell to minimize the amount of finished goods inventory it holds while still meeting customer demand in a timely manner.

Dell's Lean inventory system uses a combination of JIT and Kanban to ensure that components are available when needed without holding large quantities of raw materials or finished products. By closely managing supplier relationships and using real-time demand data, Dell has created a responsive supply chain that delivers products efficiently while minimizing inventory costs. The company's success in Lean inventory management has played a significant role in its ability to offer customized products at competitive prices.

Conclusion

Lean inventory management is a powerful approach that can significantly improve efficiency, reduce costs, and enhance customer satisfaction. By embracing the principles of Lean, such as waste reduction, JIT, and continuous improvement, businesses can streamline their inventory processes and create more agile supply chains. Tools such as 5S, Value Stream Mapping, and Kanban are essential for implementing Lean inventory management, providing businesses with the necessary means to visualize, organize, and control inventory effectively.

The success stories of Toyota, Walmart, and Dell demonstrate how Lean principles can be successfully applied across different industries to optimize inventory management. As businesses face increasing pressures to reduce costs and improve efficiency, Lean inventory management provides a proven framework for achieving these goals. By adopting Lean practices, organizations can create more efficient, cost-effective, and responsive supply chains, ultimately leading to greater competitiveness and profitability in the marketplace.

Chapter 17: Agile Inventory Strategies

Flexibility in Inventory Management

In today's fast-paced business environment, inventory management cannot afford to be rigid. Companies are often faced with fluctuating customer demands, unpredictable market conditions, and rapid technological advancements. In response to these challenges, the concept of agile inventory strategies has emerged as a critical solution to maintaining flexibility and responsiveness within the supply chain. Agile inventory management is based on the ability to quickly adapt inventory practices and processes to align with changing business needs.

At its core, flexibility in inventory management is about maintaining the ability to rapidly adjust inventory levels, order quantities, and replenishment schedules to meet demand changes. This requires businesses to foster an adaptive mindset, supported by a flexible inventory control system. Agile strategies prioritize quick responsiveness, allowing businesses to react promptly to unexpected shifts in demand, disruptions in the supply chain, and even new product launches or market trends. Unlike traditional, more rigid inventory practices that focus on static forecasts and large stockpiles, agile inventory strategies emphasize just-in-time replenishment, real-time data tracking, and continuous monitoring of inventory levels.

An agile inventory management system allows companies to manage inventory with a higher degree of control while maintaining optimal stock levels. With the ability to quickly adjust inventory levels, businesses can avoid stockouts and minimize excess inventory that leads to high carrying costs. Additionally, agile systems often rely on modern technology—such as cloud-based platforms and predictive analytics—to ensure that decision-makers have access to real-time data to make informed adjustments as demand fluctuates.

Responding to Demand Volatility

One of the most significant challenges faced by businesses is managing demand volatility. In industries such as retail, fashion, electronics, and consumer goods, demand can fluctuate dramatically based on seasonality, economic conditions, or even unanticipated events like a viral trend or supply chain disruptions. Without the ability to respond quickly to these demand shifts, businesses risk overstocking, understocking, or missing out on sales opportunities altogether.

Agile inventory strategies provide an effective framework for responding to demand volatility. This flexibility is largely driven by close collaboration with suppliers, real-time data analytics, and dynamic forecasting methods that can accommodate rapid changes in demand. For example, companies might use shorter lead times for inventory orders, allowing them to respond quickly to changes in customer preferences or sudden spikes in demand. Additionally, businesses may use safety stock buffers that are optimized in real-time to accommodate for demand surges, without overburdening the inventory system with excess stock.

Moreover, agile inventory systems also rely on regular demand forecasting reviews and updates. Instead of relying solely on historical trends, modern forecasting tools allow businesses to model potential demand scenarios, taking into account external factors such as market trends, competitor actions, and even social media signals. By leveraging this information, companies can better align their inventory strategies with volatile demand, improving their ability to fulfill customer orders on time, at competitive prices, and without excess inventory.

One practical way agile strategies can be applied to demand volatility is through **demand-driven replenishment** systems. These systems dynamically adjust inventory levels based on real-time demand signals, reducing the risk of overstocking and stockouts. Using a combination of sales data, market analytics, and predictive algorithms, businesses can continually adjust their purchasing and production cycles to match actual customer demand.

Integration of Agile Principles in Supply Chains

Agility in inventory management is closely tied to the overall agility of the supply chain. The concept of an agile supply chain is about creating a highly responsive network that can quickly adapt to changes in demand, supply, and external factors, while minimizing the risks associated with disruptions. By integrating agile principles into inventory management, companies can improve both inventory accuracy and the overall efficiency of their operations.

Key to this integration is the collaboration and communication across various supply chain stakeholders. Agile inventory strategies depend on open and transparent communication between suppliers, manufacturers, distributors, and retailers. This level of coordination helps ensure that inventory levels are balanced across the entire supply chain, with each entity reacting to changes in demand and supply as needed. The integration of suppliers into the agile process also plays a significant role in reducing lead times and improving flexibility in inventory replenishment. Businesses can quickly adjust their inventory levels by ensuring that suppliers are aligned with their changing needs, which ultimately reduces the likelihood of stockouts or excess inventory.

To facilitate this coordination, many organizations are turning to digital solutions such as **cloud-based inventory management systems** that provide a single, centralized platform for tracking inventory levels, shipments, and demand forecasts across the entire supply chain. These systems allow real-time sharing of data, which ensures that all parties are on the same page and can adjust to demand fluctuations quickly.

The application of agile principles also extends to **production scheduling**. Manufacturers are increasingly using agile production techniques that allow them to respond to shifts in demand without creating significant lead times. By using flexible manufacturing processes such as modular production systems, businesses can reconfigure production lines to meet changing customer preferences. This helps to reduce the amount of finished goods held in inventory, as companies can more easily produce items based on actual demand, rather than projected forecasts.

One important strategy in integrating agile principles into inventory management is the use of **multi-sourcing**. This approach involves working with multiple suppliers for critical materials and products, allowing businesses to mitigate risks caused by supply chain disruptions, such as natural disasters, political instability, or shortages. Multi-sourcing gives companies the ability to quickly switch suppliers or sourcing strategies in response to changing market conditions, improving the resilience and flexibility of the entire supply chain.

Additionally, businesses looking to integrate agility into their supply chain can utilize **outsourcing** strategies to achieve greater flexibility. By partnering with third-party logistics (3PL) providers or utilizing **on-demand warehousing** solutions, companies can scale up or down their storage and fulfillment operations without the need for substantial capital investment in physical assets. This scalability is a key component of agility, allowing businesses to respond to demand surges or declines without the need for long-term commitments to excess warehouse space.

Finally, **technology and automation** play a crucial role in integrating agile principles into supply chains and inventory management. The use of automation technologies, such as robotics, automated guided vehicles (AGVs), and machine learning algorithms, enables faster and more accurate inventory management, reducing lead times and increasing the overall agility of the supply chain. Automated systems can quickly identify inventory levels, identify slow-moving items, and reorder stock as needed, ensuring that the right products are always available to meet customer demand.

Agile inventory strategies also benefit from the use of **advanced data analytics**. Predictive analytics, machine learning, and AI-driven forecasting models allow businesses to anticipate demand fluctuations with greater accuracy, enabling them to adjust inventory levels in advance of potential market changes. These technologies can optimize inventory replenishment cycles, ensuring that businesses are always prepared for the unexpected without overstocking or understocking their products.

Conclusion

Agile inventory strategies are essential in today's unpredictable and fast-moving business landscape. With demand volatility and supply chain disruptions being a constant challenge, businesses must embrace flexibility and responsiveness in their inventory management practices. By adopting agile principles—such as just-in-time replenishment, demand-driven systems, multi-sourcing, and advanced digital tools—organizations can navigate these challenges while maintaining optimal inventory levels and improving customer satisfaction.

The integration of agile principles into supply chains, along with close collaboration among suppliers, manufacturers, and retailers, ensures that businesses can quickly adapt to changing demand patterns and unforeseen events. As companies continue to embrace the digital transformation of their supply chains, agile inventory management will remain a critical component in achieving operational excellence, minimizing costs, and staying competitive in the marketplace. By staying agile and responsive to change, businesses can position themselves to thrive in an ever-changing world of commerce.

Chapter 18: Hybrid Inventory Strategies

Combining Lean and Agile Approaches

In modern supply chain management, businesses are increasingly adopting hybrid inventory strategies that combine the principles of both Lean and Agile approaches. Each of these methodologies has distinct advantages: Lean focuses on minimizing waste and improving efficiency, while Agile prioritizes flexibility and responsiveness to demand fluctuations. When combined, these strategies enable businesses to create an inventory management system that not only reduces costs but also responds effectively to changes in market conditions.

The concept of a hybrid inventory strategy lies in the recognition that neither Lean nor Agile alone can fully address the complexities of contemporary supply chains. While Lean's emphasis on efficiency helps reduce excess stock and streamline operations, it can sometimes leave organizations vulnerable to demand shifts or supply chain disruptions. On the other hand, Agile's emphasis on responsiveness can result in higher costs, as companies may need to carry larger inventories or invest in quicker replenishment systems to respond to changing demand patterns.

By integrating both approaches, companies can achieve the optimal balance between cost control and the ability to quickly adapt to market changes. A hybrid approach to inventory management involves creating an inventory system that leverages the strengths of both Lean and Agile methodologies—focusing on waste reduction and efficiency in some areas, while being flexible and responsive in others.

A key feature of hybrid inventory strategies is the application of **differentiation** across inventory types. For example, products that have stable and predictable demand may be managed using Lean principles, while items with uncertain or volatile demand can be managed using Agile practices. This segmentation allows businesses to streamline operations and minimize waste in areas where it makes sense, while still maintaining the agility to meet customer needs in more unpredictable parts of the supply chain.

Balancing Efficiency and Responsiveness

One of the most significant challenges in developing a hybrid inventory strategy is balancing the often competing goals of efficiency and responsiveness. Efficiency focuses on cost reduction through processes such as inventory minimization, improved lead times, and optimized storage. On the other hand, responsiveness prioritizes the ability to quickly react to changes in customer demand, supply chain disruptions, and external market factors.

In a hybrid strategy, businesses must find ways to strike a balance between these two objectives. For example, when managing high-demand products with stable consumption patterns, Lean methods such as just-in-time inventory and demand forecasting based on historical data can be used. These products can be replenished at fixed intervals and kept in minimal quantities to avoid excess stock and reduce storage costs.

For products with more unpredictable demand, Agile strategies are more appropriate. This includes maintaining higher levels of safety stock, more frequent replenishment cycles, and shorter lead times. Agile methods also incorporate demand-driven replenishment systems, which allow companies to respond to fluctuations in real-time and adjust their inventory levels accordingly.

The key to a successful hybrid strategy lies in understanding the **demand characteristics** of different products and applying the appropriate methodology based on those characteristics. For instance, a company might use Lean techniques for its core, high-demand products that sell consistently throughout the year, while employing Agile practices for seasonal or promotional items that may experience spikes in demand at certain times.

The integration of Lean and Agile can also be facilitated through **cross-functional collaboration**. For example, the operations and procurement teams can work closely together to ensure that inventory levels align with both efficiency goals (minimizing carrying costs) and responsiveness goals (meeting customer demands). Additionally, businesses can leverage technology, such as **advanced inventory management systems**, to monitor and optimize inventory across various product categories, ensuring that efficiency and responsiveness are both considered in decision-making.

Examples of Hybrid Strategies in Practice

Many companies have successfully implemented hybrid inventory strategies, drawing on both Lean and Agile principles to navigate the complexities of modern supply chains. These examples highlight how businesses can achieve the benefits of both approaches while minimizing their respective limitations.

> **Dell's Build-to-Order Model**: Dell Computer is a prime example of a company that has successfully integrated Lean and Agile strategies into its inventory management approach. Dell's build-to-order model combines Lean manufacturing practices with Agile inventory systems to respond to customer demand efficiently. In this system, standard components are kept in inventory using Lean principles, minimizing excess stock and reducing carrying costs. However, when an order is placed, components are quickly

assembled based on the specific customer request, allowing for responsiveness to demand fluctuations. This hybrid approach enables Dell to offer custom products to customers while maintaining efficient inventory management.

Zara's Fast Fashion Supply Chain: The clothing retailer Zara is another example of a company that effectively blends Lean and Agile practices in inventory management. Zara uses Lean principles to maintain a highly efficient supply chain that minimizes lead times and stockouts for its core product lines. However, Zara also employs Agile strategies for its fast-fashion segment, where trends change rapidly, and consumer preferences can shift quickly. By maintaining flexibility and responding quickly to changes in fashion trends, Zara can replenish its stores with new styles at a pace that matches demand, minimizing the risk of overstocking while ensuring that popular items are always available.

Toyota Production System (TPS): Toyota is well-known for its Lean manufacturing system, the Toyota Production System (TPS), which focuses on eliminating waste, reducing inventory, and streamlining production. However, Toyota also incorporates Agile practices into its supply chain when it comes to managing fluctuating customer demand and supply chain disruptions. For example, Toyota utilizes a hybrid approach to inventory management, where critical components are managed with Lean principles, but other parts with uncertain demand are handled using Agile techniques, such as maintaining strategic stock and adapting production schedules to meet sudden shifts in demand.

Amazon's Inventory Management: Amazon, the e-commerce giant, uses a combination of Lean and Agile strategies to manage its vast inventory of products. For high-volume items that sell consistently, Amazon uses Lean principles to optimize storage, minimize stockouts, and reduce inventory holding costs. However, for less predictable items, Amazon uses Agile strategies, including real-time demand forecasting and quick replenishment to respond to demand spikes, seasonal fluctuations, and promotional events. By combining both approaches, Amazon can maintain its reputation for fast delivery and customer satisfaction while keeping operational costs under control.

Unilever's Hybrid Supply Chain Strategy: Unilever has adopted a hybrid supply chain model that integrates both Lean and Agile practices. For products with stable demand, such as household essentials, Unilever employs Lean techniques to minimize stock levels and streamline operations. For products with more volatile demand, such as seasonal goods or limited-edition products, Unilever uses Agile strategies, including flexible production schedules and rapid replenishment, to ensure that inventory levels are aligned with changing customer needs.

In all of these examples, the key to success lies in applying the right strategy to the right product category. Companies that have adopted hybrid inventory strategies understand the importance of **flexibility in managing different product types**. By combining Lean and Agile methodologies, these organizations have been able to achieve greater efficiency in their operations while still maintaining the ability to respond to dynamic market conditions.

Conclusion

Hybrid inventory strategies offer businesses a powerful way to manage the complexities of modern supply chains. By combining the efficiency of Lean with the responsiveness of Agile, companies can create a system that reduces costs, improves customer satisfaction, and adapts to changing market conditions. The key to success in implementing a hybrid strategy lies in understanding the characteristics of different products and applying the appropriate methodology to each. With the right balance, companies can achieve operational excellence and create a competitive advantage in an increasingly complex and fast-paced business environment.

Part 7: Leveraging Technology for Inventory Optimization

Chapter 19: ERP Systems and Inventory Management

Features of ERP Solutions

Enterprise Resource Planning (ERP) systems have become integral to modern businesses, offering comprehensive solutions to manage various functions within an organization, including inventory management. These systems are designed to centralize and automate critical business processes, ensuring seamless data flow across departments and improving decision-making efficiency. In the context of inventory management, ERP systems provide several features that enhance the visibility, control, and optimization of inventory throughout the supply chain.

One of the key features of ERP solutions is **real-time inventory tracking**, which allows businesses to monitor their stock levels continuously. By using barcodes, RFID tags, and other tracking technologies, ERP systems can provide up-to-date information on inventory movements. This real-time visibility enables companies to make informed decisions about stock replenishment, identify potential shortages, and prevent stockouts or overstocking. Moreover, it helps reduce the manual effort involved in tracking inventory, minimizing human errors and inefficiencies.

Another significant feature of ERP systems is **demand forecasting**. ERP solutions integrate historical sales data, seasonal trends, and other external factors to predict future inventory needs. Accurate demand forecasting is crucial for maintaining optimal stock levels and aligning production schedules with customer demand. By leveraging these forecasts, businesses can avoid both excess inventory, which ties up capital and storage space, and shortages that result in lost sales and customer dissatisfaction.

Inventory optimization is another powerful feature offered by ERP solutions. Modern ERP systems incorporate advanced algorithms and optimization techniques to calculate the ideal order quantities and reorder points for each product. These systems take into account factors such as lead times, order costs, and demand variability to help businesses determine the most cost-effective inventory levels. With better optimization, businesses can reduce carrying costs, minimize stockouts, and streamline their inventory replenishment processes.

ERP systems also enable **automated reorder management**, ensuring that stock is replenished automatically when inventory levels reach predefined thresholds. This automation eliminates the need for manual intervention and helps prevent overstocking or stockouts. By using ERP-driven reorder systems, businesses can create a more efficient inventory flow and respond quickly to changes in demand or supply chain disruptions.

Additionally, **inventory costing** within ERP solutions helps businesses track the financial impact of inventory movements. Through features like cost-of-goods-sold (COGS) tracking and real-time inventory valuation, ERP systems allow businesses to monitor inventory costs and assess the profitability of individual items. With precise costing data, companies can make better pricing and purchasing decisions, as well as analyze the financial health of their inventory.

Lastly, ERP systems provide **detailed reporting and analytics** tools that allow businesses to analyze their inventory performance comprehensively. These reports help organizations identify trends, detect inefficiencies, and uncover opportunities for improvement. With features such as inventory turnover analysis, ABC analysis, and stock aging reports, ERP systems provide insights that aid in decision-making and long-term strategic planning.

Integration with Inventory Operations

One of the most valuable aspects of ERP systems is their ability to **integrate with inventory operations**, streamlining processes across the entire supply chain. Integration between inventory management and other core business functions, such as procurement, sales, finance, and production, ensures that information flows seamlessly between departments, improving coordination and overall efficiency.

In terms of **procurement**, ERP systems help businesses automate purchase orders, track supplier performance, and monitor lead times. By integrating inventory data with procurement processes, businesses can ensure that they are ordering the right quantity of goods at the right time. The system can trigger automatic purchase orders when inventory levels fall below set thresholds, helping companies maintain stock levels without manual intervention. Additionally, ERP integration enables businesses to manage supplier relationships effectively by tracking orders, delivery performance, and payment schedules in real time.

The integration with **sales** operations is equally vital for inventory management. ERP systems link inventory data with sales orders, enabling businesses to track customer demand in real time. This connection helps companies avoid stockouts by automatically adjusting inventory levels based on sales trends and demand forecasts. When a customer order is placed, the ERP system can update inventory levels accordingly, ensuring that the stock is available and allocated properly.

Production and manufacturing operations also benefit from ERP integration. In manufacturing environments, ERP systems link production schedules with inventory levels, ensuring that raw materials and components are available when needed for production. This integration helps businesses avoid production delays caused by inventory shortages and optimize the use of materials. For example, if an ERP system detects that a specific raw material is running low, it can trigger a reorder process, ensuring that production continues smoothly without disruption.

Financial integration is another key aspect of ERP systems. By connecting inventory management with financial data, ERP solutions provide businesses with real-time insights into the costs associated with holding and managing inventory. These insights help finance teams track inventory costs, such as storage, insurance, and depreciation, while ensuring that inventory valuation aligns with the company's financial records. Accurate financial reporting is crucial for compliance, decision-making, and long-term strategic planning.

Supply chain visibility is enhanced when ERP systems are integrated with external partners, such as suppliers, logistics providers, and third-party vendors. With integration tools such as Electronic Data Interchange (EDI) and Application Programming Interfaces (APIs), businesses can share real-time inventory data with suppliers and logistics partners. This improves collaboration and transparency, leading to more efficient and timely deliveries. Furthermore, integration with third-party logistics providers allows businesses to track shipments in real time, providing better insights into stock levels and delivery performance.

Moreover, the integration of ERP systems with **warehouse management systems (WMS)** is critical for improving inventory accuracy and optimizing warehouse operations. WMS integration enables businesses to automate processes like order picking, packing, and shipping. It allows for more precise tracking of inventory movements within the warehouse and provides visibility into stock locations, reducing the chances of errors and improving overall warehouse efficiency.

Finally, **cloud-based ERP solutions** further enhance integration by providing access to real-time data from anywhere in the world. With cloud-based ERP, businesses can scale their operations, connect with global suppliers, and improve the flexibility of their inventory management processes. The cloud infrastructure supports seamless integration with external systems and partners, making it easier for companies to adapt to changing market conditions and supply chain challenges.

Conclusion

ERP systems play a pivotal role in modernizing inventory management by offering a comprehensive suite of features that enhance visibility, control, and optimization. By integrating inventory data with other core business functions, ERP solutions improve the accuracy and efficiency of inventory operations across the entire supply chain. From real-time tracking and demand forecasting to automated reordering and detailed analytics, ERP systems help businesses make more informed decisions, reduce costs, and maintain optimal stock levels. The integration of ERP with procurement, sales, production, and finance functions creates a seamless flow of information, ensuring that inventory management is aligned with the broader goals of the organization. As businesses continue to face complexities in inventory management, ERP solutions remain an indispensable tool for driving efficiency, improving responsiveness, and supporting long-term growth.

Chapter 20: IoT and Smart Inventory Tracking

Role of IoT in Real-Time Monitoring

The Internet of Things (IoT) has revolutionized inventory management by enabling **real-time monitoring** of inventory assets. This transformative technology allows for the continuous tracking of products, materials, and components across the entire supply chain, from the warehouse to the retail store or customer location. IoT is essentially a network of connected devices that communicate data automatically, and its application in inventory management has introduced remarkable efficiencies and capabilities that were previously unattainable.

In traditional inventory management systems, real-time visibility often depended on manual counting and human intervention, which were prone to errors and delays. However, with IoT, **sensors and smart devices** are embedded in inventory items, bins, shelves, and other storage locations. These devices are capable of gathering, transmitting, and receiving data without requiring manual input. For example, RFID (Radio Frequency Identification) tags and barcode scanners are used in combination with IoT sensors to track inventory levels, location, and condition in real time. This continuous flow of data provides a live snapshot of inventory movements and availability at any given moment.

One of the primary advantages of IoT-enabled real-time monitoring is the ability to **track inventory locations** in more granular detail. RFID tags and IoT devices can pinpoint the exact location of an item within a warehouse or distribution center, reducing the time spent searching for products and improving picking and packing accuracy. This enhanced tracking capability also extends beyond the warehouse. IoT-enabled GPS sensors can monitor the location of goods in transit, providing real-time updates on shipments and delivery status. This level of tracking enhances supply chain transparency, helping businesses respond swiftly to any disruptions or delays.

Moreover, IoT allows businesses to **automatically update inventory levels** based on product movements. As goods are moved, scanned, or shipped, the system can automatically adjust inventory counts in the backend, ensuring that the data is accurate and up to date. This helps eliminate discrepancies between physical stock levels and inventory records, a common problem with manual tracking methods. With real-time visibility, businesses can instantly detect stockouts, prevent overstocking, and optimize their reordering strategies.

In addition to monitoring physical inventory, IoT sensors can also monitor the **condition of products**, particularly those that are sensitive to environmental factors. For example, temperature and humidity sensors are used to ensure that perishable goods, such as food or pharmaceuticals, are stored within the proper conditions. This kind of environmental monitoring is critical to reducing spoilage, ensuring product quality, and meeting regulatory compliance standards.

Applications in Inventory Optimization

IoT is not only improving real-time monitoring, but it also plays a crucial role in **inventory optimization** by providing deeper insights into inventory levels, demand patterns, and operational inefficiencies. The wealth of data generated by IoT devices enables businesses to make more informed decisions, streamline processes, and reduce costs.

One of the most notable applications of IoT in inventory optimization is **demand forecasting**. By gathering real-time data on inventory movements, sales, and external factors such as weather or promotions, IoT systems can generate more accurate demand forecasts. This enables businesses to **align**

inventory levels with anticipated customer demand, ensuring that stock is neither overabundant nor insufficient. By integrating this real-time data with advanced forecasting models, companies can create highly responsive inventory management systems that reduce waste and improve service levels.

IoT also facilitates **automated reordering systems**. With sensors in place to monitor stock levels, IoT systems can automatically trigger reorder alerts when inventory reaches predefined thresholds. This minimizes the chances of stockouts and ensures that businesses never run out of popular items. Automation reduces human error and saves time, as employees no longer need to manually track inventory levels or place orders. As IoT systems communicate directly with suppliers, inventory replenishment can occur in real time, improving order accuracy and speeding up the replenishment process.

Another significant application of IoT in inventory optimization is **asset tracking and management**. In industries with high-value items or equipment, such as manufacturing or pharmaceuticals, IoT sensors are used to track the location and condition of assets. By continuously monitoring the status of these items, businesses can reduce loss, theft, and damage, which are significant sources of inefficiency and additional costs. For example, GPS sensors can help track expensive machinery or tools, ensuring that they are not misplaced and are properly maintained throughout their lifecycle. This level of tracking and management enhances operational efficiency and helps extend the life of high-cost assets.

In warehouses and distribution centers, **IoT-based systems can optimize the storage layout and material handling** processes. By analyzing the real-time data provided by IoT sensors, companies can assess which products are frequently accessed and which are rarely moved. This data helps optimize warehouse layouts by positioning high-demand items in easily accessible locations, thereby reducing picking time and increasing overall operational efficiency. IoT-enabled smart shelving can also automatically adjust to accommodate varying product sizes, improving storage density and reducing wasted space.

Condition-based maintenance is another important application of IoT in inventory optimization. IoT sensors can monitor the health of inventory storage systems, such as refrigeration units, conveyor belts, or forklifts. By gathering real-time data on equipment performance, businesses can perform **predictive maintenance**—addressing potential failures before they occur—thus avoiding costly downtime and minimizing the risk of inventory spoilage. This proactive maintenance approach ensures the continuous flow of operations and reduces the likelihood of unforeseen disruptions in the supply chain.

IoT also contributes to **improving supplier and customer relationships**. By integrating IoT data with supplier and customer portals, businesses can share real-time inventory updates and status reports. For instance, suppliers can be alerted when stock levels reach reorder points, ensuring timely restocking of goods. Similarly, customers can receive accurate and up-to-date information about product availability, leading to improved satisfaction and trust. Enhanced communication through IoT creates a more transparent and responsive supply chain, benefiting both suppliers and customers.

Additionally, IoT-based systems can be integrated with **advanced analytics and artificial intelligence (AI)** tools to generate actionable insights. Through machine learning algorithms, businesses can identify patterns and trends in inventory data, which can be used to optimize stock levels, forecast demand, and plan for future growth. AI-powered predictive analytics can provide deeper insights into which items are likely to experience high demand or low sales, helping businesses make smarter inventory decisions and reduce costly stockouts or overstocks.

Furthermore, IoT technology can be combined with **blockchain** to enhance the traceability and transparency of inventory movements across the supply chain. By recording inventory data on a secure and immutable ledger, companies can create an auditable trail of every transaction, improving trust among partners and ensuring compliance with regulations. Blockchain integration allows businesses to verify the authenticity of goods, track their provenance, and mitigate the risk of fraud, particularly in industries like food and pharmaceuticals, where safety and quality are critical.

Conclusion

IoT and smart inventory tracking have fundamentally transformed the way businesses manage and optimize their inventory. By enabling real-time monitoring, improving demand forecasting, automating reordering, and enhancing asset management, IoT technology offers unprecedented levels of efficiency and insight. The data collected by IoT devices empowers businesses to make better-informed decisions, reduce costs, and enhance customer satisfaction. Furthermore, by integrating IoT with advanced analytics, AI, and blockchain, organizations can unlock even greater potential in inventory optimization, supply chain transparency, and overall operational performance. As IoT continues to evolve, its impact on inventory management will only grow, making it an indispensable tool for modern businesses striving to stay competitive in an increasingly dynamic market.

Chapter 21: AI and Machine Learning in Inventory Optimization

Predictive Inventory Analytics

Artificial Intelligence (AI) and Machine Learning (ML) have emerged as powerful tools in the field of inventory optimization, offering businesses the ability to enhance efficiency and accuracy through predictive analytics. At its core, **predictive inventory analytics** leverages advanced algorithms and vast amounts of historical data to forecast future demand with remarkable precision. This capability is particularly important in inventory management, where understanding future demand trends is crucial for maintaining optimal stock levels, avoiding stockouts, and minimizing excess inventory.

Predictive analytics begins with the collection of historical sales data, stock levels, seasonal trends, and even external factors such as weather patterns, promotions, and market events. AI and ML models then process this data, identify patterns, and generate demand forecasts based on a variety of inputs. These forecasts provide inventory managers with actionable insights into when and how much to order, which products will experience increased demand, and which ones might face a decline. For example, AI systems can analyze past sales performance and seasonal trends to predict spikes in demand for products, allowing businesses to increase stock levels in anticipation of these fluctuations.

By using AI-powered forecasting techniques, companies can reduce the risk of stockouts and overstocking. Traditional methods of demand forecasting often rely on simple averages or manual adjustments, which can be error-prone and ineffective in a volatile market. AI, on the other hand, continuously learns from new data, improving the accuracy of its predictions over time. **Machine learning algorithms** are particularly adept at handling complex datasets, recognizing subtle correlations between various factors, and adapting to changes in demand behavior. This results in more accurate and dynamic inventory management, which is crucial for maintaining optimal stock levels while minimizing carrying costs.

In industries with unpredictable demand patterns, such as fashion or technology, AI and ML-based predictive analytics can be game-changers. By analyzing vast amounts of data, including social media trends, customer preferences, and competitor activity, AI systems can predict which products will be in high demand. This level of insight allows businesses to stock their inventory more efficiently, avoiding overproduction of low-demand items and ensuring they meet consumer expectations with high-demand products.

Beyond simply predicting demand, predictive inventory analytics also extends to **supply chain forecasting**. AI can identify potential disruptions or bottlenecks in the supply chain by analyzing factors like supplier performance, lead times, and geopolitical events. This allows businesses to proactively adjust their inventory strategies, mitigate risks, and avoid delays. Predictive analytics can even optimize replenishment cycles by identifying the optimal reorder points based on forecasted demand, thereby reducing the likelihood of excess inventory and improving the overall efficiency of the supply chain.

Another powerful application of predictive analytics is in **inventory optimization across multiple locations**. AI models can evaluate the demand for specific products across different geographical locations, helping businesses adjust stock levels based on regional preferences and sales trends. This enables companies to **distribute inventory more efficiently**, ensuring that high-demand products are available where they are needed most, while minimizing the risk of stockouts or overstocking at less-demanded locations.

Automation in Decision-Making

While predictive analytics provides businesses with invaluable insights into demand patterns, **automation in decision-making** takes inventory optimization to the next level by enabling real-time, data-driven actions without human intervention. AI and ML play a crucial role in automating inventory-related decisions, from replenishment orders to stock transfers between warehouses, reducing the need for manual oversight and increasing operational efficiency.

AI-powered systems can automatically determine the optimal inventory levels for each product based on real-time data, eliminating the need for manual recalculations and human judgment. For example, an AI system can continuously monitor inventory levels and automatically trigger a reorder when stock reaches a predefined threshold. This automation ensures that businesses can maintain adequate stock without having to rely on periodic inventory checks or guesswork. By integrating these AI-powered systems with **enterprise resource planning (ERP)** or **warehouse management systems (WMS)**, companies can create a seamless flow of data that enables smarter, automated decision-making across the entire inventory management process.

Dynamic pricing strategies are another area where AI and machine learning play a pivotal role in inventory optimization. AI algorithms can evaluate multiple factors, such as inventory levels, demand forecasts, competitor pricing, and customer behavior, to adjust product prices dynamically in real-time. For example, if a certain product is overstocked, AI systems can automatically lower the price to accelerate sales and reduce inventory. Conversely, if demand is forecasted to rise for a particular item, AI can suggest price increases to maximize profit margins. These automated pricing adjustments help businesses remain competitive while optimizing their inventory turnover.

In the context of **order fulfillment**, AI and machine learning can automate decisions related to stock allocation. For instance, AI systems can evaluate the geographic location of customers, the availability of stock in various warehouses, and delivery lead times to automatically choose the optimal fulfillment center for each order. This reduces shipping costs, improves delivery speed, and ensures that products are shipped from the closest warehouse with available stock. Furthermore, machine learning algorithms can help identify the most efficient packing methods, improving both speed and cost-effectiveness in the fulfillment process.

Automated decision-making extends to **inventory replenishment**. Rather than relying on manual inputs to place restocking orders, AI systems can continuously monitor sales patterns and forecast demand to place automated orders with suppliers. These systems can factor in lead times, supplier performance, and economic conditions, ensuring that the right quantity of inventory is replenished at the right time. As a result, businesses can reduce the likelihood of stockouts or excess inventory, optimize supplier relationships, and streamline their entire supply chain.

AI can also **optimize warehouse management** by automating stock transfers and order picking. Through machine learning models, AI can identify the most efficient routes for picking and packing orders based on real-time stock availability, warehouse layout, and order priorities. Additionally, AI systems can monitor and adjust inventory storage based on product demand patterns, ensuring that high-demand items are stored in easily accessible locations and reducing the time spent searching for products.

One of the most compelling aspects of automation in decision-making is its ability to respond quickly to **supply chain disruptions**. Whether caused by natural disasters, supplier delays, or unforeseen demand spikes, AI systems can rapidly analyze real-time data and adjust inventory strategies in response to these disruptions. By automatically identifying alternative suppliers, adjusting reorder quantities, or redistributing stock across locations, businesses can maintain optimal inventory levels even in the face of uncertainty.

Conclusion

AI and machine learning are transforming inventory optimization by enabling more accurate demand forecasting, automating decision-making, and improving overall efficiency in inventory management. Predictive inventory analytics powered by AI allows businesses to forecast demand with unprecedented accuracy, while automation reduces human intervention and streamlines processes like replenishment, order fulfillment, and stock allocation. By leveraging AI's ability to analyze vast datasets and make real-time decisions, companies can improve inventory turnover, reduce costs, and respond to changing market conditions with agility. As AI and machine learning technologies continue to evolve, their integration into inventory management will further enhance operational efficiency, providing businesses with a powerful toolkit to optimize their inventory and stay competitive in a rapidly changing marketplace.

Part 8: Sustainability and Risk Management

Chapter 23: Sustainable Inventory Practices

Green Supply Chain Strategies

Sustainability has become a central focus in modern supply chain management, driven by the need to reduce environmental impact, meet consumer demand for eco-friendly practices, and adhere to stricter regulatory requirements. Sustainable inventory management is a critical component of a **green supply chain**, as it directly influences the amount of waste generated, energy consumed, and resources utilized across various stages of the supply chain. In particular, **green supply chain strategies** focus on reducing carbon footprints, minimizing waste, and optimizing resource utilization throughout the inventory management process.

One of the primary green strategies is to optimize **inventory turnover**. Holding excessive stock not only ties up capital but also increases the environmental burden of storing, transporting, and potentially disposing of unsold goods. By minimizing overstocking, businesses can reduce the environmental footprint associated with storage and handling, such as energy consumption in warehouses and transportation emissions. In addition, reducing excess inventory helps minimize the waste generated from expired, damaged, or unsold products, which often end up in landfills, contributing to environmental harm.

A **key approach** in implementing green supply chain strategies is the integration of **sustainable sourcing** and **eco-friendly materials**. Businesses can work closely with suppliers who adopt sustainable practices, such as using renewable resources, reducing packaging waste, or ensuring that the materials are recyclable. This approach can significantly reduce the environmental impact of inventory management, from raw materials to finished products. For example, choosing materials that are biodegradable or made from recycled content can help reduce the carbon footprint of the final product and enhance the sustainability of the overall supply chain.

Circular supply chain practices are also becoming increasingly popular, where the focus shifts from a linear "take-make-dispose" model to a circular "reuse-repair-recycle" model. In this context, businesses can design products that are easy to disassemble and recycle, reducing the need for virgin materials and minimizing waste at the end of the product lifecycle. For inventory management, this means incorporating **reverse logistics** to bring back used products or packaging for reuse, recycling, or refurbishment, thereby minimizing the amount of waste generated during the product lifecycle.

Moreover, **collaboration with stakeholders** across the supply chain plays a crucial role in implementing green practices. By engaging suppliers, logistics providers, and customers in sustainability efforts, businesses can establish practices that reduce the environmental impact across the entire supply chain. For example, working with logistics partners to optimize delivery routes and minimize fuel consumption, or adopting more energy-efficient warehouse practices, can significantly contribute to a greener supply chain.

The role of **green technologies** cannot be overlooked either. For instance, implementing advanced technologies such as **cloud-based inventory management systems** enables businesses to track real-time inventory levels, improve forecast accuracy, and better align supply with demand, reducing the need for overproduction and minimizing waste. Additionally, **Internet of Things (IoT)** sensors can help monitor temperature-sensitive goods to ensure products are stored optimally, preventing spoilage and reducing waste, especially in industries like food and pharmaceuticals.

Reducing Inventory Waste

The issue of **inventory waste** is one of the most pressing concerns in inventory management, especially in industries where products have a limited shelf life or where large quantities of unsold stock end up as waste. Waste in inventory management is not just an economic burden; it also poses a significant environmental problem, contributing to increased landfill waste and higher levels of energy consumption for the disposal of excess products. **Reducing inventory waste** is thus a key objective for businesses that want to improve sustainability and reduce their environmental footprint.

A **critical strategy** for reducing inventory waste is the implementation of **just-in-time (JIT) inventory management**. JIT focuses on reducing excess stock by ensuring that products are ordered and received only as they are needed for production or sale. This approach minimizes storage requirements and prevents the accumulation of unsold goods, thereby reducing waste and environmental impact. JIT inventory management relies heavily on accurate demand forecasting, efficient supply chain processes, and strong supplier relationships to ensure that products arrive at the right time and in the right quantity.

Demand-driven inventory management further complements JIT by aligning inventory levels with actual customer demand rather than anticipated demand. By using **predictive analytics**, companies can better forecast demand and adjust their inventory levels accordingly. This reduces the risk of overstocking products that are unlikely to sell, thereby decreasing the chances of excess inventory and the waste associated with unsold products.

Product lifecycle management (PLM) also plays a vital role in reducing waste. PLM helps companies track products from their inception to disposal, identifying opportunities for reusing, refurbishing, or recycling materials and components. This strategy is particularly important for industries such as electronics, where products have short life cycles, and the disposal of electronic waste (e-waste) has become a growing environmental concern. By incorporating PLM into inventory management, companies can reduce waste by promoting the reuse of materials and improving recycling rates.

Inventory consolidation is another approach that reduces waste by ensuring that businesses maintain fewer, more strategic stock locations rather than overstocking across multiple sites. This not only minimizes the environmental footprint of operating multiple warehouses but also optimizes the flow of goods, reducing the need for unnecessary transportation and storage. Through consolidation, businesses can better control inventory levels and improve stock rotation practices to avoid products reaching their expiration date.

The concept of **product obsolescence** also directly relates to inventory waste. Obsolescence occurs when products become outdated or no longer sell due to changing customer preferences, technological advancements, or other factors. To mitigate this risk, businesses can implement **inventory rationalization** strategies, which involve regularly reviewing and assessing inventory across multiple locations and products. This helps identify slow-moving or obsolete items, allowing businesses to phase out these products and avoid accumulating waste.

Technology plays a significant role in **reducing inventory waste** by enabling businesses to make better data-driven decisions. **Artificial intelligence (AI)** and **machine learning (ML)** can optimize demand forecasting, reducing the likelihood of overstocking and understocking. By analyzing large datasets, AI can identify patterns and trends that may not be immediately obvious to human planners, leading to more accurate predictions of future demand. These technologies also allow for dynamic adjustments to inventory levels in real time, helping businesses react quickly to shifts in demand and market conditions.

Another significant tool in minimizing waste is the use of **barcoding and RFID technology**. These technologies allow for the real-time tracking of inventory throughout the supply chain, from the warehouse to the customer. By providing accurate and timely information about stock levels and product movement, businesses can reduce the risk of products sitting idle in warehouses for extended periods, which could lead to waste or obsolescence.

Collaboration with customers is also a powerful strategy in reducing inventory waste. By understanding customer behavior and collaborating closely with them on demand forecasting, businesses can ensure that products are being ordered and stocked in quantities that align with actual consumption, minimizing the chances of overproduction and excess inventory. Offering **take-back programs** or **product return initiatives** can also help reduce waste by encouraging customers to return unused products for refurbishment or recycling.

Conclusion

Sustainable inventory practices are not just about reducing waste and environmental impact; they are about creating more efficient, cost-effective, and socially responsible supply chains. By adopting green supply chain strategies, businesses can reduce their carbon footprint, minimize waste, and optimize the use of resources throughout the entire inventory lifecycle. Through methods such as just-in-time inventory, demand-driven management, product lifecycle management, and inventory consolidation, companies can reduce waste and improve inventory efficiency. Additionally, leveraging advanced technologies like AI, IoT, and RFID can further enhance sustainability efforts while improving inventory forecasting and management processes. Ultimately, businesses that prioritize sustainable inventory practices are not only contributing to a greener planet but also gaining a competitive advantage in an increasingly environmentally-conscious marketplace.

Chapter 24: Risk Management in Inventory Optimization

Identifying and Mitigating Risks

Inventory optimization is a delicate balancing act between meeting customer demand and minimizing the costs associated with holding and managing inventory. However, this process is fraught with potential risks that can significantly affect both operational efficiency and profitability. Effective risk management in inventory optimization is essential to ensure that businesses can navigate uncertainties, avoid stockouts or overstocking, and maintain a steady flow of goods in a dynamic supply chain environment.

One of the primary risks in inventory management is **demand variability**. Fluctuations in customer demand, whether due to seasonal changes, market trends, or unforeseen events like economic downturns or changes in consumer behavior, can lead to inventory imbalances. **Underestimating demand** can result in stockouts, missed sales opportunities, and dissatisfied customers, while **overestimating demand** can lead to excess inventory, tying up capital, increasing holding costs, and potentially leading to waste if products become obsolete or expire. To mitigate this risk, businesses must adopt accurate demand forecasting methods and continuously monitor real-time data to adjust inventory levels accordingly.

Another significant risk is **supply chain disruptions**, which can occur due to various factors such as natural disasters, geopolitical instability, supplier failures, transportation delays, or global health crises like pandemics. These disruptions can affect the availability and cost of raw materials or finished goods, leading to delays in production or fulfillment and creating significant inventory challenges. To mitigate the impact of supply chain disruptions, businesses must develop strong relationships with multiple suppliers, create **alternative sourcing strategies**, and maintain **buffer**

stocks for critical products to cushion the impact of disruptions.

Inventory shrinkage due to theft, damage, or mismanagement is another risk that businesses must account for. Shrinkage reduces the accuracy of inventory counts and undermines efforts to optimize inventory levels. Implementing **robust security measures**, such as surveillance systems, access controls, and regular audits, can help minimize this risk. Additionally, investing in **advanced inventory management technologies**, such as RFID tags or barcode scanning systems, can provide real-time visibility into inventory movement and help identify discrepancies before they become significant problems.

Rising costs in raw materials, labor, and transportation also present significant risks to inventory optimization. Fluctuations in these costs can erode profit margins and complicate inventory management efforts. For example, a sudden increase in fuel prices can lead to higher transportation costs, while labor shortages may delay product manufacturing or delivery. To address these risks, companies can negotiate long-term contracts with suppliers to lock in prices, explore alternative transportation options, or invest in automation technologies to reduce labor dependency.

Contingency Planning for Disruptions

No matter how well inventory optimization strategies are designed, disruptions are inevitable, and having a **contingency plan** in place is crucial for minimizing their impact. A contingency plan outlines the steps a business will take to respond to unforeseen events or risks that disrupt normal operations, helping to reduce recovery time and ensure the continuity of supply chain processes.

A well-structured **contingency plan** for inventory optimization involves **identifying potential risks** and creating predefined actions to mitigate their impact. The first step in developing such a plan is to conduct a thorough **risk assessment** across the supply chain. This assessment should consider various scenarios, including natural disasters, supplier bankruptcies, transportation strikes, economic fluctuations, and technological failures. By identifying and categorizing risks based on their probability and potential impact, businesses can prioritize their contingency planning efforts.

One critical component of a contingency plan is the establishment of **buffer inventory** or **safety stock**. While safety stock is a regular part of inventory management, it becomes even more important in the context of risk management. Businesses must determine the appropriate level of safety stock based on factors such as lead times, demand variability, and the criticality of certain products. Having additional stock on hand can help mitigate the impact of sudden demand spikes or supply chain disruptions. However, businesses should balance the benefits of safety stock with the associated costs of holding excess inventory, ensuring that it does not undermine efforts to reduce overall inventory levels.

Diversifying suppliers is another key strategy for managing risks in inventory optimization. Relying on a single supplier for critical components or products creates a vulnerability in the supply chain. If that supplier experiences issues, such as a factory fire or transportation strike, it can cause severe disruptions to inventory flow. To mitigate this risk, businesses should develop relationships with multiple suppliers and, where possible, source materials from different geographical regions. This not only reduces the reliance on any single supplier but also helps companies remain agile and responsive in the face of disruptions.

Technology plays a significant role in contingency planning for inventory optimization. Modern inventory management systems, such as **Enterprise Resource Planning (ERP)** software or **Supply Chain Management (SCM)** systems, provide real-time visibility into inventory levels, demand patterns, and supply chain activities. These systems can help identify potential issues before they escalate, allowing businesses to take corrective action promptly. For example, if inventory levels are running low due to a supplier delay, the system can trigger an alert, prompting the procurement team to take action, such as seeking alternative suppliers or expediting orders.

Furthermore, **automated reorder systems** can help businesses stay ahead of potential inventory shortages, reducing the reliance on manual processes that are prone to error. By automating the reorder process based on predefined thresholds, companies can ensure that inventory is replenished before it reaches critical levels, preventing stockouts and minimizing the need for emergency orders during disruptions.

Another essential part of contingency planning is developing **communication protocols** for emergencies. In the event of a disruption, clear and efficient communication with suppliers, distributors, and customers is critical. Businesses should establish emergency contact lists and ensure that key personnel are trained to respond swiftly and effectively to disruptions. Regular communication with suppliers, particularly during periods of uncertainty, can help companies stay informed about potential supply chain risks, such as transportation delays or raw material shortages.

In addition to **internal preparedness**, businesses should also consider the role of **collaboration and partnerships** in risk management. In the face of supply chain disruptions, working together with partners and suppliers can create more resilient and flexible systems. For example, some suppliers may be able to support expedited deliveries, while logistics providers can offer alternative routes in case of transportation bottlenecks. By fostering strong relationships with stakeholders across the supply chain, businesses can leverage their networks and resources to minimize the impact of disruptions.

Finally, businesses should regularly **review and update** their contingency plans. As supply chains evolve, new risks emerge, and changes in market conditions or technology can alter the risk landscape. By continuously reassessing potential risks and updating contingency plans accordingly, businesses can ensure that their inventory management systems remain agile and responsive to the challenges of the modern supply chain.

Conclusion

Effective risk management in inventory optimization requires businesses to be proactive and adaptable in the face of uncertainty. Identifying potential risks, such as demand variability, supply chain disruptions, and inventory shrinkage, and implementing strategies to mitigate them is essential for maintaining smooth operations and minimizing the financial impact of disruptions. Equally important is the development of a comprehensive **contingency plan** that includes strategies such as maintaining buffer inventory, diversifying suppliers, leveraging technology, and fostering strong relationships with partners. By preparing for potential disruptions and ensuring that inventory management systems are agile and responsive, businesses can safeguard their operations, enhance customer satisfaction, and remain competitive in an increasingly unpredictable business environment.

Part 9: Specialized Topics in Inventory Management

Chapter 25: Inventory Metrics and KPIs

Key Performance Indicators (KPIs)

In the fast-paced and highly competitive world of inventory management, measuring performance is critical to ensure efficiency, reduce costs, and improve service levels. Key Performance Indicators (KPIs) are vital tools for businesses to assess their inventory management processes and understand how well they are meeting their goals. KPIs are quantifiable metrics that help organizations evaluate various aspects of their inventory performance, such as turnover rates, order fulfillment accuracy, and overall inventory accuracy. By regularly monitoring these indicators, companies can make informed decisions to optimize inventory levels, improve profitability, and enhance customer satisfaction.

A wide range of KPIs can be used to evaluate inventory performance. Some of the most common and effective KPIs in inventory management include:

> **Inventory Turnover Ratio**: This KPI measures how often a company sells and replaces its inventory over a specific period. It is calculated by dividing the cost of goods sold (COGS) by the average inventory value during that period. A high turnover rate indicates that the company is efficiently selling and replenishing inventory, while a low turnover rate may suggest slow-moving stock or overstocking.
>
> **Stockouts and Backorders**: The frequency of stockouts or backorders reflects the ability of a company to meet customer demand without delays. A high number of stockouts or backorders can lead to dissatisfied customers and lost sales, which can significantly impact the bottom line. This KPI highlights

areas where inventory levels may need to be adjusted or where forecasting needs improvement.

Order Fulfillment Cycle Time: This metric tracks the time it takes from receiving an order to the final shipment. A shorter cycle time typically indicates an efficient inventory management system with fast-moving stock, while a longer cycle time may point to issues such as stockouts, poor warehouse organization, or inefficient order picking.

Carrying Costs of Inventory: Carrying costs are the expenses associated with holding inventory, including storage, insurance, obsolescence, and taxes. This KPI helps companies assess the impact of excess inventory on profitability. By reducing carrying costs, businesses can free up capital for other investments or operations.

Fill Rate: The fill rate measures the percentage of customer orders that are completely filled without backorders or stockouts. A high fill rate indicates a well-maintained inventory system capable of meeting demand promptly. A low fill rate may suggest the need for better inventory planning, more efficient reordering practices, or improved supplier relationships.

Gross Margin Return on Investment (GMROI): GMROI calculates the profit generated by each dollar invested in inventory. It is an essential KPI for understanding the profitability of inventory investments. A higher GMROI means that inventory is contributing positively to overall profitability, while a lower GMROI signals that inventory is not generating the desired returns.

Inventory Accuracy and Shrinkage Rates

Inventory Accuracy is a key metric for assessing the precision of inventory data. It reflects how closely the actual inventory matches the recorded stock levels in the system. Accurate inventory counts are critical for making informed decisions, minimizing stockouts and overstocking, and ensuring optimal inventory levels. Inaccurate inventory records can lead to several issues, such as poor order fulfillment, excess carrying costs, and ultimately dissatisfied customers.

Maintaining high inventory accuracy requires a combination of **regular stocktaking** and the use of **advanced inventory management systems** (IMS). There are several approaches to improving inventory accuracy, including cycle counting, periodic audits, and leveraging technologies like **barcoding**, **RFID**, and **real-time tracking systems**. Automated systems that provide real-time inventory updates are essential in reducing manual errors and improving accuracy.

Inventory Shrinkage refers to the loss of inventory due to theft, damage, or administrative errors. It is often expressed as a percentage of the total inventory and represents the discrepancy between the recorded stock levels and the actual stock on hand. Shrinkage can have a significant impact on profitability, especially if it is not adequately controlled.

To minimize shrinkage, businesses must adopt a multi-pronged approach. This includes implementing robust **security measures**, such as CCTV surveillance, restricted access to storage areas, and employee training on handling inventory carefully. Regular **inventory audits** are also essential to detect shrinkage early and to identify areas where controls may be lacking. In addition, investing in **automated tracking technologies**, such as RFID, can help companies detect discrepancies in real time, reducing the chances of inventory theft or damage going unnoticed.

Benchmarking Best Practices

Benchmarking is a valuable practice that allows businesses to compare their inventory management performance against industry standards or best-in-class competitors. By identifying where they stand relative to others in the same field, businesses can gain valuable insights into potential areas for improvement and adopt industry-leading practices. Benchmarking involves analyzing various inventory-related metrics and KPIs, such as inventory turnover, lead time, and carrying costs, to identify gaps in performance.

There are several approaches to benchmarking inventory management performance. **Internal benchmarking** involves comparing inventory metrics across different departments, regions, or locations within the same company. This can highlight inefficiencies or best practices that can be shared across the organization. **External benchmarking** compares a company's performance with industry peers or competitors. External benchmarks may be obtained from industry reports, surveys, or trade associations.

One of the most effective benchmarking strategies is to focus on the **best practices** in the industry. These practices often result from years of experience, technological advancements, and continuous improvement efforts by leading companies in the field. Some of the best practices in inventory management include:

> **Adopting Just-In-Time (JIT) inventory systems**: JIT minimizes inventory levels by aligning production and delivery schedules with customer demand. This reduces carrying costs and the risk of overstocking while improving cash flow. However, JIT requires

accurate demand forecasting and reliable suppliers to ensure that products are available when needed.

Implementing automated inventory tracking systems: As mentioned earlier, adopting technologies like **RFID**, **barcode scanning**, and **warehouse management systems** (WMS) can significantly improve inventory accuracy and reduce human error. These technologies provide real-time visibility into inventory levels and enhance stock tracking, order fulfillment, and demand forecasting.

Leveraging demand forecasting: Accurate demand forecasting enables businesses to better match supply with customer demand, avoiding both stockouts and overstocking. Advanced forecasting methods, such as **machine learning** and **predictive analytics**, can help companies improve forecast accuracy by analyzing historical data and predicting future trends more accurately.

Optimizing reorder points and safety stock levels: By calculating the right reorder points and maintaining appropriate safety stock levels, businesses can prevent stockouts without overinvesting in inventory. Reorder point analysis takes into account lead times, order quantities, and demand variability to determine the optimal levels of stock to keep on hand.

Streamlining warehouse operations: Best-in-class companies often invest in optimizing their warehouse layouts and operations to minimize lead times and reduce inventory handling costs. This includes improving **picking efficiency**, reducing order cycle times, and minimizing errors in order fulfillment. Efficient warehouses enable faster inventory turnover and reduce the risk of excess stock.

Collaboration with suppliers: Building strong relationships with suppliers can help businesses ensure a consistent flow of inventory, reduce lead times, and negotiate better terms. Collaborative supply chain strategies, such as **vendor-managed inventory** (VMI), can also help optimize stock levels by allowing suppliers to manage inventory replenishment directly.

By integrating these best practices into their inventory management strategy, companies can gain a competitive edge, reduce costs, and improve customer satisfaction. Regular benchmarking ensures that businesses remain agile and responsive to industry changes, helping them stay ahead of the competition.

Conclusion

Inventory management is a critical function within any organization, and understanding key performance indicators (KPIs), maintaining inventory accuracy, and benchmarking against best practices are essential steps for optimizing performance. KPIs like inventory turnover, order fulfillment cycle time, and gross margin return on investment provide valuable insights into inventory performance and can guide businesses toward more effective decision-making. Similarly, managing inventory accuracy and shrinkage rates is key to maintaining efficient and cost-effective inventory systems. Finally, benchmarking allows organizations to measure their performance against industry leaders, adopt best practices, and continuously improve their inventory management strategies. By effectively managing these aspects of inventory, companies can achieve greater operational efficiency, reduce costs, and enhance customer satisfaction.

Chapter 26: Managing Non-Moving and Slow-Moving Inventory

Identifying Non-Moving Inventory

Non-moving inventory refers to items that have remained unsold or unused for a prolonged period. These items often take up valuable storage space, tie up working capital, and contribute to the overall inefficiency of inventory management. Identifying non-moving inventory is critical to improving inventory turnover, reducing carrying costs, and ensuring that resources are allocated efficiently across products that drive sales or are essential for production. The challenge with non-moving inventory is that it can go unnoticed for long periods unless businesses have proper systems in place to track and monitor inventory performance.

There are several key indicators that help identify non-moving inventory:

> **Ageing Inventory Reports**: One of the most common ways to spot non-moving inventory is by using ageing reports, which categorize inventory based on how long it has been sitting in storage. These reports help identify items that have been in stock for longer than a predetermined period, indicating that they are not moving. Items in the "overstocked" or "obsolete" categories are typically good candidates for closer evaluation.

> **Inventory Turnover Ratio**: By calculating the inventory turnover ratio, businesses can identify which items are moving slowly. A low turnover ratio for certain products suggests that those items are not selling as quickly as others. This ratio helps pinpoint the specific products that contribute to high inventory holding costs without providing corresponding sales value.

Sales Data and Demand Forecasting: A detailed analysis of historical sales data can highlight items with consistently low sales. Comparing this data with the forecasted demand can reveal discrepancies, indicating that certain products are not in line with the expected sales cycle. A mismatch between actual demand and forecasted sales helps identify slow-moving inventory.

Stock Replenishment Patterns: Non-moving inventory can often be identified through irregular replenishment patterns. When products consistently do not meet reorder points or have long periods of inactivity in terms of restocking, it is a sign that they are not moving.

Product Lifecycle and Obsolescence: Some items naturally have a limited lifecycle, especially in industries like technology, fashion, or food. Products that are nearing the end of their life cycle may be harder to sell or may no longer be in demand. Recognizing these patterns early can help manage slow-moving or obsolete stock.

Strategies to Reduce Excess Stock

Managing excess stock involves both short-term and long-term strategies aimed at improving cash flow, reducing carrying costs, and optimizing storage space. Excess stock often occurs when businesses overestimate demand, fail to accurately forecast sales, or neglect proper inventory control. Reducing excess inventory requires a combination of process improvements, better forecasting, and strategic decision-making.

Several effective strategies can help reduce excess stock:

Improved Demand Forecasting: A key way to prevent excess stock is by improving demand forecasting accuracy. By using historical sales data, market trends, and predictive analytics, businesses can better align their purchasing and replenishment cycles with actual customer demand. Accurate forecasts help avoid overordering and reduce the risk of holding excess inventory that may not sell.

Dynamic Inventory Replenishment: Adopting a dynamic replenishment strategy ensures that inventory levels are continuously adjusted based on real-time demand signals. Inventory levels can be adjusted more frequently, reducing the chances of accumulating excess stock. A Just-In-Time (JIT) or Lean inventory system allows businesses to replenish stock only when necessary, minimizing the likelihood of excess or obsolete items building up.

Implementing Inventory Optimization Techniques: Utilizing techniques such as **ABC Analysis, Reorder Point (ROP) calculations**, and **Safety Stock Management** can help businesses manage their inventory more effectively. By classifying products into categories based on their sales volume and profitability, businesses can prioritize fast-moving, high-margin products and minimize overstocking of low-demand items.

Vendor-Managed Inventory (VMI): In some cases, businesses can collaborate with suppliers to implement **Vendor-Managed Inventory** systems, where the supplier manages the stock levels at the company's premises. Suppliers have access to inventory data and sales forecasts, allowing them to replenish inventory only when necessary, thereby reducing the chances of excess stock accumulating.

Stock Rotation and First-In, First-Out (FIFO): Ensuring that older stock is used or sold first is an essential method for reducing excess stock. Implementing **FIFO** or **LIFO** (Last-In, First-Out) can help prevent older inventory from becoming obsolete and reduce the chances of overstocking items that are slow to move. Stock rotation ensures that the oldest items are always prioritized, keeping the stock fresh and reducing the need for clearance sales or discounts.

Bundling Products: Combining slow-moving items with fast-moving products in promotional bundles can help move excess stock. Customers are often more willing to buy a bundle that provides additional value.

This strategy can help businesses clear out inventory that has been sitting idle for some time.

Reducing Lead Times: Shortening lead times with suppliers can help avoid excess stock buildup. By improving supplier relationships and negotiating better lead times, businesses can order stock more frequently and avoid ordering too much at once. This strategy helps manage stock levels more dynamically and reduce excess inventory.

Collaborative Forecasting: Collaborating with suppliers and other stakeholders to improve forecasting accuracy can help businesses align their orders with demand. Sharing sales data, trends, and inventory reports with suppliers allows for more synchronized replenishment and reduces the need for excess stock.

Disposal and Reuse Approaches

While reducing excess stock and managing slow-moving inventory is crucial, it's inevitable that some products may still need to be disposed of or repurposed. Disposal and reuse strategies help businesses minimize financial losses and environmental impact. There are several methods for handling slow-moving or obsolete stock:

Discounting and Clearance Sales: One of the most common ways to clear out excess stock is through discounted pricing or clearance sales. Offering significant discounts can encourage customers to purchase slow-moving products. This helps recover some of the costs associated with holding the inventory while freeing up storage space.

Liquidation: For items that are no longer in demand or have become obsolete, liquidation can be a practical solution. Companies can sell off excess stock to liquidators, who will sell it at a reduced price or to other markets where it may still have demand. While the company may not recover its full value from liquidation, it helps recover some capital and frees up warehouse space.

Donations: In some cases, businesses may choose to donate non-moving inventory to charitable organizations. This not only helps clear out stock but can also result in tax deductions, depending on local laws and regulations. Donations are a socially responsible way to manage excess stock and contribute to the community.

Recycling or Repurposing: Products that can no longer be sold might still have value in other forms. Businesses can look into recycling or repurposing non-moving inventory by breaking it down into components or materials that can be used for other purposes. For example, electronics that are obsolete may be dismantled for parts and sold to refurbishers.

Repackaging or Refurbishing: For certain products, repackaging or refurbishing can be an effective way to bring them back into the market. Items that are still functional but have become outdated or damaged can be repaired, refurbished, or repackaged into new configurations that appeal to different customer segments. This approach can help recover some of the value from excess stock.

Donation to Employees: In some companies, slow-moving or obsolete stock is offered to employees at discounted prices or for free. This method provides employees with useful items while helping the business reduce its inventory levels.

Composting or Waste Disposal: For products that have reached the end of their lifecycle and cannot be sold, donated, or repurposed, proper disposal methods, including composting or waste disposal, are necessary. Businesses must ensure that this process is done in an environmentally responsible manner, complying with regulations on waste management.

Conclusion

Effectively managing non-moving and slow-moving inventory is essential to optimizing storage space, reducing carrying costs, and improving cash flow. Identifying non-moving inventory through tools such as ageing inventory reports and sales data analysis is the first step in mitigating excess stock. Once identified, businesses can implement strategies to reduce excess stock, including improved forecasting, dynamic replenishment, inventory optimization techniques, and better collaboration with suppliers. In situations where excess stock cannot be avoided, various disposal and reuse methods, such as liquidation, discounting, and recycling, can help minimize financial losses and environmental impact. By employing these strategies, businesses can maintain leaner inventory levels, improve operational efficiency, and maintain profitability in a highly competitive marketplace.

Chapter 27: Raw Material Aging Reports and Burn-Off Reports

Using Aging Reports for Inventory Decisions

Aging reports are vital tools for managing raw materials in inventory, particularly when it comes to tracking items that have been in storage for extended periods. These reports categorize inventory based on how long items have been held in stock, highlighting which raw materials are nearing expiration or becoming obsolete. The use of aging reports in inventory management can drive informed decisions that improve cash flow, reduce waste, and enhance overall inventory efficiency.

Aging reports typically divide inventory into time-based categories, such as 0-30 days, 31-60 days, 61-90 days, and so on. By assessing the age of raw materials within these intervals, businesses can identify materials that may soon become unusable or unsellable. This proactive approach helps prevent the accumulation of obsolete or expired materials and reduces the risk of financial loss due to materials that no longer meet quality standards.

Using aging reports for inventory decisions offers several key benefits:

Prioritizing Consumption of Older Materials: One of the primary advantages of aging reports is that they enable inventory managers to prioritize the use of older raw materials. This ensures that older materials are consumed first, preventing them from becoming wasted or obsolete. Prioritizing aging stock can help improve inventory turnover and reduce the need for write-offs due to expired or outdated materials.

Improved Stock Rotation: Aging reports play a key role in stock rotation practices such as FIFO (First In,

First Out). By using the information provided in aging reports, businesses can ensure that raw materials are consumed in the correct order, preventing older stock from sitting idle. Implementing FIFO can significantly reduce the chances of materials becoming obsolete, especially for those with a limited shelf life, such as food ingredients or chemicals.

Forecasting and Replenishment Decisions: Aging reports provide valuable insights into inventory patterns that can be used for forecasting future material requirements. By analyzing the rate at which materials are used and their aging patterns, businesses can better anticipate when new stock will be needed and plan replenishments accordingly. This can help minimize excess inventory buildup, improve cash flow, and ensure that the right raw materials are available when needed.

Identifying Overstocking Issues: Aging reports can help highlight raw materials that have been overstocked or are not moving at the expected rate. Items that remain in inventory longer than expected could indicate that the business has overestimated demand, leading to excess stock. This can also be a sign that certain materials are not being used as planned, which might require adjustments to production schedules or marketing strategies.

Minimizing Waste and Obsolescence: An aging report provides a clear picture of which materials are nearing the end of their useful life. For example, in industries such as pharmaceuticals, chemicals, or food production, raw materials may have an expiration date, and those nearing that date need to be used first. Aging reports allow businesses to identify materials at risk of becoming waste and take action to avoid unnecessary losses by utilizing them promptly.

Optimizing Supplier Relationships: By sharing aging reports with suppliers, businesses can encourage better communication regarding the shelf life and delivery schedules of raw materials. This transparency can help improve the timing of deliveries to prevent the receipt of materials that are already close to expiration or overstocking of raw materials. Supplier relationships become more efficient when both parties understand the aging status of materials.

Regulatory Compliance: In certain industries such as food, pharmaceuticals, or chemicals, regulatory requirements mandate the use of materials within specific timeframes. Aging reports can help ensure that businesses comply with these regulations by preventing the use of expired or outdated raw materials. This can reduce the risk of costly fines, recalls, or safety incidents due to the use of non-compliant materials.

Cost Control: By accurately identifying slow-moving or aging inventory, businesses can make more informed decisions about their purchasing and production processes. Preventing overstocking or investing in materials that have a high likelihood of becoming obsolete can significantly reduce waste-related costs. Aging reports can help businesses negotiate better pricing with suppliers by eliminating the need for excess stock and the associated storage and handling costs.

Burn-Off Reports in Reducing Waste

A burn-off report is an essential tool for monitoring the consumption of raw materials in relation to production schedules. This report tracks the quantity of materials used over a specific period, providing insights into material utilization and identifying potential waste reduction opportunities. The term "burn-off" refers to the process of using raw materials until they are fully consumed, and a burn-off report helps businesses optimize this process by offering visibility into usage patterns.

Burn-off reports are particularly useful for industries with materials that have a limited shelf life, such as food and beverage, pharmaceuticals, or chemicals. These reports allow businesses to monitor and control how quickly materials are being used, ensuring that no raw materials sit idle and become obsolete.

The role of burn-off reports in reducing waste includes several key benefits:

Improved Resource Utilization: Burn-off reports enable businesses to track the consumption rate of raw materials in real-time, helping to identify inefficiencies in the production process. By comparing actual usage with forecasted requirements, businesses can pinpoint areas where materials may be overused or underutilized. This insight allows for adjustments in the production process to ensure that materials are being consumed efficiently, reducing waste and improving overall resource utilization.

Reducing Overstocking: By aligning burn-off rates with inventory levels, businesses can better predict when to reorder raw materials and avoid overstocking. Overstocking raw materials increases the risk of excess inventory, leading to more waste and higher storage costs. Burn-off reports help businesses maintain an optimal balance between supply and demand, reducing the likelihood of over-purchasing and minimizing waste.

Managing Expiring Materials: For industries with materials that expire or degrade over time, burn-off reports help businesses manage the timely use of these items. Materials that are at risk of expiration can be prioritized for use, ensuring that they are consumed before they lose their effectiveness or become unsellable. This helps businesses reduce losses associated with expired materials and optimize inventory turnover.

Optimizing Production Scheduling: Burn-off reports provide valuable data for production planning and scheduling. By understanding the rate at which raw materials are consumed, businesses can adjust production schedules to better align with material usage. This ensures that production is continuous, but raw material waste is minimized, and storage space is effectively utilized. More accurate production schedules help prevent delays and shortages, leading to more efficient operations.

Identifying and Addressing Material Waste: Burn-off reports help businesses identify instances where materials are being wasted due to inefficiencies in production or handling. For example, excess scraps, spills, or improperly mixed materials may be leading to higher levels of waste. By regularly monitoring burn-off data, businesses can pinpoint sources of waste and take corrective action, such as improving training, optimizing equipment, or adjusting handling procedures.

Cost Control and Waste Reduction: A major advantage of burn-off reports is their ability to help businesses control costs associated with raw material waste. By accurately tracking material usage and minimizing waste, businesses can reduce their raw material costs, improve profitability, and pass on savings to customers. This is especially important for industries with high raw material costs, where waste reduction efforts directly contribute to cost savings.

Promoting Sustainable Practices: Burn-off reports can play a role in sustainability initiatives by helping businesses minimize raw material waste and reduce their environmental footprint. Using materials more efficiently reduces the amount of waste that needs to be disposed of, contributing to a more sustainable business model. For example, in food production, ensuring that raw ingredients are used efficiently and without unnecessary waste can help lower the environmental impact of production processes.

Inventory Replenishment Optimization: Burn-off reports provide insight into material consumption patterns that can be used to optimize inventory replenishment cycles. By understanding how quickly raw materials are being burned off, businesses can more accurately predict when they will need to reorder and avoid stockouts. This helps maintain a consistent production flow while preventing the accumulation of excess stock.

Conclusion

Both aging and burn-off reports are integral tools in the raw material management process. Aging reports help businesses identify materials that are at risk of becoming obsolete or wasted, enabling them to take proactive steps to use or dispose of them before they lose value. Burn-off reports, on the other hand, track the consumption of raw materials and provide insights into how well materials are being utilized in the production process. By using these reports, businesses can optimize their raw material inventory, reduce waste, improve efficiency, and contribute to overall cost control and sustainability efforts. Properly leveraging aging and burn-off reports is an essential component of effective inventory management in industries with perishable or time-sensitive raw materials.

Chapter 28: Combining ABC and XYZ Analysis

Benefits of Integrated Analysis

When it comes to optimizing inventory management, combining ABC and XYZ analysis provides a more comprehensive approach to categorizing and managing inventory. While each of these methodologies offers valuable insights on its own, their integration can significantly enhance decision-making, forecasting accuracy, and stock control. ABC analysis categorizes inventory based on the value of items, while XYZ analysis assesses the variability in demand. By combining these two techniques, businesses can create a more dynamic inventory management system that aligns both with cost considerations and demand fluctuations. The integrated approach enables organizations to apply the right level of attention and resources to different inventory segments, optimizing both efficiency and profitability.

One of the primary benefits of combining ABC and XYZ analysis is that it enables businesses to take into account both the value of their inventory items and the predictability of their demand. For example, ABC analysis helps prioritize items based on their cost or sales importance, categorizing them into A, B, and C groups. However, ABC alone doesn't take into account the variability in demand patterns, which is crucial for managing supply chain risks. By integrating XYZ analysis, which categorizes items based on their demand variability (X for stable, Y for moderate, and Z for erratic), businesses gain a more nuanced understanding of inventory needs.

For example, high-value items that exhibit stable demand (categorized as A-X items) are typically considered a priority for inventory management because they contribute significantly to overall sales or profitability and are consistently in demand. In contrast, low-value items with erratic demand (C-Z items) might require a different inventory strategy, such as reduced stock levels and increased flexibility in replenishment.

By combining these two methodologies, companies can gain better insights into:

> **Inventory Prioritization**: Businesses can more effectively prioritize inventory items based on both their value and the predictability of demand. High-value items with stable demand should be given priority in terms of stock levels and replenishment strategies, while lower-value or volatile demand items might be managed with just-in-time (JIT) strategies to reduce excess stock and minimize holding costs.
>
> **Optimized Stock Levels**: With the integrated analysis, businesses can determine optimal stock levels for each category. For instance, high-value items with unpredictable demand (A-Z) may require more frequent monitoring and adjustments to minimize both stockouts and excess inventory. This provides a more tailored inventory management approach, ensuring that resources are allocated appropriately.

Improved Forecasting and Replenishment: The integrated approach enhances demand forecasting by incorporating both the value of items and their demand patterns. Items in the "A" or high-value category with erratic demand can benefit from advanced forecasting models, while "C" or low-value items with stable demand may require more basic forecasting methods. This allows businesses to plan more accurately and minimize the risk of stockouts or overstocking.

Reduced Inventory Costs: By accurately understanding demand patterns and item importance, businesses can optimize storage costs, transportation, and inventory holding costs. This also aids in minimizing capital tied up in low-turnover items, allowing for better cash flow management. Integrating ABC and XYZ analysis allows businesses to streamline their supply chains by reducing unnecessary inventory while ensuring critical items are always available.

Better Risk Management: With the combined approach, businesses can identify high-risk inventory items that need to be managed carefully. For example, high-value items with unpredictable demand (A-Z) may pose a higher risk in terms of potential loss or obsolete stock. These risks can be mitigated by implementing more frequent reviews, agile replenishment systems, and contingency planning.

Strategies for Implementation

Integrating ABC and XYZ analysis into an inventory management system requires a strategic approach to ensure that both methodologies are effectively combined and applied to the right inventory segments. The following strategies can help businesses implement an integrated ABC-XYZ analysis framework:

Segment Inventory by Value and Demand Variability: Start by conducting both ABC and XYZ analyses separately. For the ABC analysis, categorize inventory based on criteria such as sales volume, revenue contribution, or the cost of goods sold. Similarly, for the XYZ analysis, evaluate demand patterns for each item over a period, classifying them into stable (X), moderate (Y), and erratic (Z) categories. Once both analyses are complete, overlay the results to assign each inventory item to an ABC-XYZ combination category. For example, an item could be classified as A-X (high value, stable demand) or C-Z (low value, erratic demand).

Determine Appropriate Inventory Strategies for Each Category: Once inventory items have been classified according to their ABC-XYZ categories, assign tailored inventory management strategies to each group. For A-X items, for example, focus on ensuring high availability and consistency by maintaining appropriate stock levels, implementing safety stock, and using more sophisticated forecasting methods. For C-Z items, which are low-value and have erratic demand, employ JIT systems, lean inventory techniques, and reduced stock levels to minimize holding costs. Implementing different strategies for each category allows businesses to align their inventory practices with both cost-effectiveness and demand requirements.

Leverage Technology for Automation: Implementing integrated ABC-XYZ analysis can be a complex task without the use of modern inventory management systems. Leverage enterprise resource planning (ERP) or specialized inventory management software to automate the process of classification and monitoring of inventory. Many ERP systems offer built-in tools to help categorize inventory items based on both their value and demand volatility, automatically updating classifications based on real-time data and forecasts. This reduces the manual effort required and ensures that inventory strategies are always aligned with current demand and stock conditions.

Regularly Update Classifications: The classification of inventory items should not be static. Demand patterns and product values change over time due to factors such as market trends, seasonality, and product life cycles. Regularly reviewing and updating the ABC-XYZ classifications ensures that businesses are always using the most relevant and up-to-date information to guide inventory decisions. Establish a routine for periodically reviewing inventory data and making necessary adjustments to ensure that the inventory management strategies remain aligned with the evolving business environment.

Train Staff and Build Awareness: Successful implementation of an integrated ABC-XYZ analysis requires that all relevant staff members understand its importance and how it impacts inventory management. Provide training on how to use both ABC and XYZ data, and communicate how these insights will inform decision-making in areas such as procurement, forecasting, and replenishment. This ensures that staff members are equipped to manage inventory more effectively and contribute to the overall efficiency of the supply chain.

Use Forecasting and Demand Planning Models: To fully leverage the benefits of combining ABC and XYZ analysis, businesses should integrate forecasting and demand planning models into the process. High-value items (A) with stable demand (X) may require more accurate and long-term forecasting models, while low-value items (C) with erratic demand (Z) may require more responsive, short-term models. By adjusting forecasting methods based on both the value and variability of demand, businesses can enhance the accuracy of their replenishment strategies and avoid unnecessary stockouts or excess inventory.

Monitor and Adjust as Needed: Once the integrated ABC-XYZ framework is implemented, it is essential to continuously monitor inventory performance and adjust strategies as needed. Regularly analyze key performance indicators (KPIs) such as inventory turnover, stockouts, and carrying costs to ensure that inventory management practices are working effectively. Adjust stock levels, forecasting models, and procurement strategies as required to ensure that inventory remains aligned with demand and value requirements.

Conclusion

Combining ABC and XYZ analysis offers a powerful, integrated approach to inventory management that allows businesses to balance both value and demand variability when making critical decisions. The benefits of this integrated analysis are numerous, from better inventory prioritization and optimized stock levels to improved forecasting and reduced inventory costs. By implementing strategic measures such as leveraging technology, training staff, and regularly updating classifications, businesses can optimize their inventory management processes, improve supply chain performance, and maximize profitability. The integration of ABC and XYZ analysis enables businesses to create a more dynamic and efficient inventory management system that not only minimizes costs but also responds proactively to market fluctuations and customer demand.

Part 10: The Future of Inventory Optimization

Chapter 29: Emerging Trends in Inventory Management

Predictive Analytics and Real-Time Optimization

The landscape of inventory management is undergoing a transformative shift, largely driven by advancements in technology. Among the most influential trends shaping the future of inventory optimization are predictive analytics and real-time optimization. These technologies are enabling companies to forecast inventory needs with unprecedented accuracy, streamline operations, and reduce costs. Predictive analytics refers to the use of historical data, machine learning models, and statistical algorithms to forecast future inventory demands, while real-time optimization uses data collected in real time to adjust inventory levels and operations dynamically.

The integration of predictive analytics in inventory management allows businesses to anticipate future demand patterns based on a variety of factors such as past sales, market conditions, seasonal trends, and even external variables like weather or geopolitical events. By accurately predicting demand, companies can avoid overstocking, reduce excess inventory, and minimize stockouts, ensuring that the right products are available at the right time. Predictive models can also be fine-tuned over time, improving their accuracy and effectiveness as more data becomes available.

Real-time optimization takes this concept a step further by continuously adjusting inventory levels and order quantities based on real-time data inputs. For example, inventory systems connected to point-of-sale systems can track the movement of products as they are sold, allowing businesses to make immediate adjustments to reorder levels or stock placement. This enables businesses to respond quickly to demand fluctuations, prevent inventory shortages, and improve customer satisfaction. Real-time optimization also extends to supply chain processes, such as routing deliveries or adjusting shipping schedules to ensure timely replenishment and minimize stockouts.

Both predictive analytics and real-time optimization are invaluable in the context of today's fast-paced, globalized economy. They empower businesses to operate more efficiently, reduce costs, and enhance service levels. Companies that adopt these technologies will have a competitive edge, as they can make more informed, data-driven decisions and respond swiftly to changes in the market.

Autonomous Warehousing and Robotics

Another emerging trend in inventory management is the adoption of autonomous warehousing and robotics. As businesses seek to reduce operational costs, improve efficiency, and increase scalability, automation technologies are playing an increasingly prominent role in modern supply chains. Autonomous systems, including automated guided vehicles (AGVs), drones, and robotic process automation (RPA), are being deployed to streamline warehousing operations and improve inventory management.

Autonomous warehousing systems are designed to automate a variety of tasks within the warehouse, including product picking, sorting, packaging, and delivery. Automated guided vehicles (AGVs) can transport goods throughout the warehouse, reducing the need for manual labor and minimizing human error. These vehicles are often equipped with advanced sensors and machine learning algorithms, allowing them to navigate complex environments, avoid obstacles, and optimize their travel paths. This enhances both the speed and accuracy of warehouse operations.

Robotic picking systems are also revolutionizing how inventory is managed. These robots can be programmed to identify, pick, and pack items from shelves with high precision. In combination with real-time inventory tracking systems, robotic picking reduces the time spent locating and retrieving items, improves order accuracy, and accelerates order fulfillment. Furthermore, robotics can be used for inventory counts and shelf scanning, which not only ensures inventory accuracy but also reduces the need for manual stocktaking, a process that is often time-consuming and error-prone.

Drones are increasingly being employed for inventory management and warehouse operations as well. Drones equipped with RFID and barcode scanning technology can fly through warehouses to scan and update inventory in real time. This eliminates the need for manual stocktaking and helps improve inventory accuracy. The ability to perform inventory counts in a fraction of the time it would take manually allows for more frequent and thorough inventory updates, which is crucial for efficient stock management.

Beyond their immediate operational benefits, autonomous warehousing systems contribute to greater supply chain resilience. By reducing dependency on human labor, companies can mitigate the risks associated with workforce shortages or labor disruptions. Automation also facilitates scalability, enabling businesses to manage growing inventory volumes without significant increases in labor costs.

The integration of robotics into warehousing operations is also enhancing safety. Robots can handle heavy lifting, hazardous materials, and repetitive tasks, reducing the risk of workplace injuries. In an environment where safety is critical, the automation of these tasks helps create a safer working environment for employees.

As autonomous warehousing systems continue to evolve, they are becoming more sophisticated and capable of performing an even broader range of tasks. In the near future, it is likely that fully automated warehouses, where robots and AI systems control every aspect of the inventory management process, will become increasingly commonplace.

The Future Outlook for Inventory Optimization

The future of inventory optimization lies at the intersection of emerging technologies, data-driven decision-making, and agile supply chains. Predictive analytics and real-time optimization are already providing businesses with greater visibility and control over their inventory, and as these technologies advance, their capabilities will only continue to improve. By harnessing the power of these tools, companies will be able to further optimize inventory levels, reduce costs, and enhance customer satisfaction.

Similarly, the rise of autonomous warehousing and robotics is transforming the way inventory is managed within warehouses and distribution centers. Automation is driving efficiency, scalability, and safety, while simultaneously reducing the reliance on manual labor. As these technologies become more advanced and accessible, the future of inventory management will be marked by increased automation, real-time data-driven decision-making, and a seamless integration between the physical and digital supply chains.

The integration of these emerging trends presents new challenges and opportunities for businesses. Companies will need to invest in training and reskilling their workforce to ensure that employees are equipped to work alongside automated systems. Additionally, organizations will need to prioritize cybersecurity and data privacy as they collect and share more real-time data across the supply chain. With careful planning and strategic implementation, businesses can navigate these challenges and harness the full potential of these technologies to stay competitive in an increasingly complex and dynamic market.

In conclusion, the future of inventory optimization is set to be shaped by the continued evolution of predictive analytics, real-time optimization, autonomous warehousing, and robotics. These technologies promise to revolutionize inventory management, providing businesses with the tools they need to improve efficiency, reduce costs, and enhance customer satisfaction. As businesses continue to adapt and innovate, inventory optimization will remain a key driver of success in the global supply chain landscape.

Chapter 30: Preparing for the Next Generation of Inventory Challenges

Adapting to Technological Shifts

As the global marketplace becomes increasingly dynamic and interconnected, the landscape of inventory management is evolving rapidly. Traditional methods that once formed the backbone of inventory systems are now being challenged by new, more sophisticated technologies. In this context, preparing for the next generation of inventory challenges means not just keeping pace with technological innovations but proactively leveraging them to stay ahead.

The first major technological shift reshaping inventory management is the rise of artificial intelligence (AI) and machine learning (ML). These technologies have the potential to dramatically enhance the accuracy and efficiency of inventory forecasting, demand planning, and stock replenishment. AI can process vast amounts of data from multiple sources, identifying patterns and predicting trends that are beyond human capacity to discern. This allows businesses to anticipate demand more accurately, reduce excess inventory, and avoid stockouts. Machine learning algorithms, in particular, can continuously improve over time, refining their predictions and recommendations based on real-time data and changing market conditions.

Another technological advancement that is transforming inventory management is the Internet of Things (IoT). IoT technology enables real-time tracking of inventory and assets through connected sensors, RFID tags, and smart devices. These technologies provide visibility across the entire supply chain, from the warehouse to the point of sale. This real-time data stream allows businesses to monitor inventory levels and movement with unprecedented precision. IoT also facilitates proactive inventory management by alerting teams to potential issues such as understocked shelves, product expirations, or goods in transit that are delayed. The integration of IoT with other systems like ERP platforms creates a seamless flow of information, enabling automated decision-making processes and a more efficient supply chain.

Cloud-based systems are also playing a pivotal role in modern inventory management. The flexibility and scalability offered by cloud computing allow businesses to access real-time data and collaborate more effectively across geographically dispersed locations. Cloud platforms enable centralized data management, which improves accuracy and consistency in inventory records. Furthermore, the cloud provides a secure environment for storing large volumes of data, which can be leveraged for better decision-making and predictive analytics.

Blockchain technology is another emerging force in inventory management. While still in its early stages, blockchain promises to enhance supply chain transparency and traceability. With its ability to create an immutable ledger, blockchain can ensure that inventory records are tamper-proof and that all transactions are transparent and verifiable. This is especially crucial for industries where the provenance and authenticity of products are critical, such as pharmaceuticals and luxury goods. By integrating blockchain with inventory management systems, businesses can improve trust and reduce fraud while streamlining operations.

The next generation of inventory management will also see the widespread adoption of robotic process automation (RPA) and robotics in warehousing. Automated systems, such as drones for inventory counting and autonomous mobile robots (AMRs) for material handling, are revolutionizing how warehouses operate. These technologies reduce the reliance on human labor for repetitive tasks, improve operational efficiency, and help maintain a higher degree of accuracy. Additionally, advanced robots can assist in picking, packing, and sorting goods, enhancing throughput and reducing the time it takes to fulfill orders.

In preparation for these technological shifts, organizations must invest in upgrading their technological infrastructure and ensure that their workforce is equipped to manage and work alongside these advanced tools. This involves fostering a culture of continuous learning, where employees are encouraged to develop their skills in emerging technologies, data analytics, and automation. Businesses should also consider partnerships with tech innovators to stay at the forefront of developments in inventory management.

Building Resilient and Agile Supply Chains

The need for resilient and agile supply chains has never been more pressing, particularly in the wake of disruptions such as the COVID-19 pandemic, geopolitical uncertainties, and climate-related events. A resilient supply chain is one that can withstand shocks and continue to operate effectively, even in the face of unforeseen events. An agile supply chain, on the other hand, is one that can quickly adapt to changes in demand, supply, and market conditions. Together, these qualities are essential for organizations to maintain competitive advantage and meet customer expectations in an increasingly volatile environment.

Building a resilient and agile supply chain starts with creating a flexible inventory management system that can respond swiftly to demand fluctuations and supply disruptions. This means shifting away from traditional, rigid models of inventory control and embracing systems that can accommodate variability. The use of real-time data, driven by technologies like IoT, AI, and machine learning, is critical in achieving this flexibility. By having access to up-to-date information on inventory levels, supplier performance, and customer demand, businesses can make informed decisions quickly and adjust their inventory strategies as needed.

Another critical aspect of building resilience is the diversification of suppliers and distribution channels. Relying on a single supplier or a small group of suppliers exposes businesses to significant risks if one of these suppliers faces a disruption. By diversifying the supplier base, organizations can mitigate the impact of such disruptions and ensure that they have alternative sources of supply. Similarly, maintaining multiple distribution channels and logistics partners helps businesses maintain access to customers, even if one channel faces delays or closures.

In addition to diversification, it is crucial for businesses to establish strong relationships with their suppliers. Collaborative relationships built on trust and mutual benefit enable businesses to work closely with suppliers to address challenges, share information, and innovate solutions together. This level of collaboration enhances the agility of the supply chain, as suppliers are more likely to respond quickly to changes in demand or supply when there is a strong partnership in place.

Another strategy for building a resilient supply chain is the development of contingency plans for potential disruptions. This includes identifying the risks that could impact inventory availability, such as natural disasters, transportation strikes, or political instability, and creating plans to address them. For example, businesses might create emergency stockpiles for critical items, establish backup suppliers, or implement dual sourcing strategies to ensure that they can continue operations even if one supplier or source of inventory is compromised.

Technology also plays a key role in building supply chain resilience. Advanced forecasting tools powered by AI and machine learning can help businesses anticipate future disruptions and plan accordingly. For instance, predictive analytics can identify emerging trends in supply chain disruptions, allowing companies to take preventive measures before a crisis unfolds. Additionally, supply chain visibility platforms enable businesses to track the status of orders, shipments, and inventory in real-time, providing them with the insights needed to make quick adjustments when things go wrong.

Agility in inventory management is about being able to respond to changes in demand or supply with minimal delay. One way to achieve this agility is by adopting flexible inventory strategies such as just-in-time (JIT) or demand-driven replenishment models. These strategies enable businesses to minimize inventory levels while still ensuring that they can meet customer demand. However, implementing these strategies requires an in-depth understanding of customer behavior and market trends. Companies must rely on accurate forecasting, effective demand sensing, and close collaboration with suppliers to ensure that they can meet changing demand without overstocking.

An agile supply chain also requires the ability to scale quickly in response to spikes in demand. For example, during periods of unexpected surges in demand, businesses must have the capacity to quickly ramp up production, adjust inventory levels, and expand distribution capabilities. The use of flexible manufacturing systems, automated warehouses, and dynamic distribution networks can support this scalability.

At the heart of both resilience and agility is the ability to make data-driven decisions. Businesses must invest in systems and technologies that can collect, analyze, and visualize data from across the supply chain. With access to accurate and timely data, companies can identify bottlenecks, inefficiencies, and risks in their inventory and supply chain processes and take proactive measures to address them. This data-driven approach not only enhances decision-making but also fosters a culture of continuous improvement, where businesses are constantly optimizing their supply chain operations to meet evolving customer needs.

Conclusion

As we look toward the future, the next generation of inventory management will be characterized by rapid technological advancements and an increased focus on supply chain resilience and agility. The technologies of today—such as AI, IoT, cloud computing, and robotics—will become even more integral to inventory management, enabling businesses to operate with greater precision, speed, and flexibility. At the same time, organizations must focus on building supply chains that can withstand disruptions and quickly adapt to changes in demand and supply.

To prepare for the challenges of the future, businesses must invest in the right technologies, develop strong supplier relationships, embrace flexible inventory strategies, and create a culture of continuous improvement. By doing so, they can build inventory systems that not only meet the demands of today's fast-paced market but also position themselves to thrive in an increasingly unpredictable and competitive global landscape.

Conclusion

Recap of Key Concepts and Strategies

Throughout this book, we have explored the intricate world of inventory management, highlighting the core principles, strategies, and technologies that are essential for optimizing inventory systems. We have delved into the various methods for categorizing inventory, with an emphasis on how to effectively classify, forecast, and control stock levels to meet dynamic demand and reduce excess inventory. The integration of advanced technologies such as AI, IoT, ERP systems, and machine learning has been central to the discussions, showcasing how these innovations enhance accuracy, efficiency, and decision-making across the inventory lifecycle.

One of the foundational concepts we've discussed is the importance of strategic inventory control. This involves balancing inventory to ensure product availability while minimizing costs. Techniques like the Economic Order Quantity (EOQ), safety stock management, and reorder systems—such as Kanban and Min-Max—are crucial in maintaining the optimal flow of goods. Alongside these, lean and agile strategies have proven valuable in adapting to market changes, eliminating waste, and responding swiftly to demand fluctuations.

Furthermore, we have explored advanced inventory models such as multi-echelon inventory optimization and the application of the Newsvendor model for perishable goods, which allow businesses to fine-tune their operations to meet specific needs across diverse product categories. The importance of inventory forecasting, using both qualitative and quantitative methods, has been emphasized to ensure accurate predictions that align with inventory goals.

As sustainability becomes an increasingly significant concern, the book highlighted practices to reduce inventory waste and minimize environmental impact. From green supply chain strategies to risk management and contingency planning, it's clear that the future of inventory management must prioritize both operational efficiency and environmental responsibility.

The application of KPIs and metrics in inventory management has also been a key focus. By using precise indicators to track performance, businesses can continuously assess and refine their inventory strategies to improve accuracy, reduce shrinkage, and enhance overall efficiency. Moreover, specialized tools like raw material aging reports and the combination of ABC and XYZ analysis have proven invaluable in identifying slow-moving inventory, allowing companies to make more informed decisions about stock rotation, disposal, and reallocation.

Finally, we explored the future trends of inventory management, with an emphasis on adapting to technological shifts and building resilient, agile supply chains. The growing importance of data-driven decision-making, supported by advanced analytics, real-time monitoring, and automated systems, positions inventory professionals to stay ahead in a rapidly evolving global marketplace.

The Path Ahead for Inventory Professionals

As the field of inventory management continues to evolve, inventory professionals must be ready to navigate a rapidly changing landscape. The convergence of technological advancements and the increasing complexity of global supply chains presents both challenges and opportunities for those in the profession. To thrive in this environment, inventory professionals must focus on the following key areas:

First, staying informed about the latest technological advancements is essential. Professionals should invest in continuous learning and adapt their skill sets to incorporate emerging technologies. Mastery of tools like AI, IoT, and blockchain will be crucial, as these technologies increasingly drive efficiency, accuracy, and transparency in inventory management. Professionals should also seek to leverage data analytics to gain insights into inventory performance, customer behavior, and market trends.

Next, inventory professionals must continue to embrace flexibility and agility. As market conditions fluctuate, the ability to quickly adjust inventory levels, source alternative suppliers, and adapt to changes in customer demand will differentiate successful organizations from those that struggle to keep up. The integration of lean, agile, and hybrid strategies will be paramount in achieving this flexibility. Agile methodologies will allow companies to respond to disruptions with speed, while lean principles will help reduce waste and streamline operations.

Another critical area is the strengthening of supply chain resilience. The ability to mitigate risks associated with inventory management is increasingly important. Professionals should focus on building contingency plans, diversifying suppliers, and developing robust tracking and monitoring systems. Creating a resilient inventory system that can adapt to unforeseen disruptions—such as pandemics, natural disasters, or geopolitical challenges—will be essential for maintaining business continuity.

Collaboration will also play an integral role in the future of inventory management. As supply chains become more interconnected, inventory professionals will need to work closely with other departments, such as procurement, logistics, and IT, to optimize the entire inventory ecosystem. Building strong relationships with suppliers and leveraging data sharing across the value chain will foster a collaborative environment that enhances decision-making and operational efficiency.

Finally, sustainability will continue to shape the future of inventory management. Inventory professionals should be proactive in adopting green practices and finding ways to reduce the environmental impact of inventory systems. By minimizing waste, optimizing stock levels, and promoting sustainable sourcing, inventory managers can contribute to broader corporate sustainability goals.

In conclusion, the path ahead for inventory professionals is one of continuous innovation and adaptability. By staying ahead of technological trends, embracing new methodologies, strengthening supply chains, and prioritizing sustainability, professionals in this field will play a key role in helping organizations navigate the complexities of modern inventory management. As businesses increasingly rely on their inventory systems to drive operational efficiency and customer satisfaction, the role of the inventory professional will continue to evolve, offering exciting opportunities for growth and impact in the years to come.

www.ingramcontent.com/pod-product-compliance
Lightning Source LLC
Chambersburg PA
CBHW071022240526
45469CB00006BD/2039